Unprovoked Murder
(Insanity or Demon Possession?)

Unprovoked Murder
(Insanity or Demon Possession?)

by
Dr. Lester Sumrall

SUMRALL PUBLISHING
South Bend, Indiana

Unless otherwise indicated, all Scripture quotations are taken from the *King James Version* of the Bible.

Unprovoked Murder
(Insanity or Demon Possession?)
ISBN 1-58568-198-9
(This book is a compilation of *Unprovoked Murder*, formerly registered as ISBN 1-89274-202-X, and *Hostility*, formerly registered as ISBN 0-8407-5765-4.)
Copyright © 1999 by
Sumrall Publishing
P. O. Box 12
South Bend, IN 46624

Contents

Introduction

We can pick up any newspaper these days, and find stories of technological advances. New discoveries in the medical and nutritional fields, which can afford people a healthier and longer life. Low inflation, low interest rates and record low unemployment rates, evidences of a booming economy. So many things in our Country are going so right. It's an exciting time to live.

However, in that same newspaper there will undoubtedly be stories that can fill the reader with disgust and dread. Stories of gruesome, senseless murders. Kids mercilessly killing kids in school. Shootings of toddlers at Day Care Centers, diners in restaurants and of innocent, hard working people in office buildings. Drive-by shootings, road-rage. Even the senseless killing of worshipping young people in a place we have always considered safe, a church building.

What a contrast, on one hand, we seem to live in a land of plenty. There's good all around us. There's growth, scientific breakthroughs, prosperity and opportunity. On the other hand there's an ever-present evil that appalls us with its indiscriminate destruction of innocent lives.

When we hear of such indiscriminate and senseless murders, our hearts ache for the victims and we ask, "Why do these things happen?"

There is one problem that stands out above others in our land in these times: the problem of unprovoked murder.

Unprovoked murder. What is it?

In using the term, *unprovoked murder*, I mean a brutal act in which one person destroys another person (or persons) for no apparent reason. The victim is either a stranger to him or a person with whom he has had no quarrel. He kills only because of a compulsion within him. It says, "Destroy," so he destroys. Oftentimes these brutal acts of destruction involve the innocent lives of women, children, and the elderly.

Through the centuries, there have been many cases of unprovoked murder, but today there is a dreadful acceleration of such crimes. Violent crime is increasing at a speed we cannot tolerate in our land.

For many years it seemed the serious murder cases that we read about were always off somewhere in a big city — New York or San Francisco or Los Angeles. Today, they are in your hometown and mine. Statistics show that one out of every three American families have been touched by crime.

Why does one human being murder another?

Unprovoked murder has become an enigma to the legal and judicial authorities. For judges, attorneys, and juries of criminal courts, it seems that the easy way out is to issue a verdict of "insanity."

What does *insanity* mean?

Is unprovoked murder *insanity*? Or is it *demon possession*?

These questions must be dealt with. We cannot just sit by and watch as humans destroy other humans. That time is past.

In the following pages, I attempt to answer these questions. I urge you to read these words with a heart that is open to the truth. The subject is not pleasing; but to reach a solution, you must be willing to face the problem. *Unprovoked Murder — Is It Insanity or Demon Possession?*

Go with me now, and let's find the answer.

Lester Sumrall

Unprovoked Murder
(Insanity or Demon Possession?)

1
Unprovoked Murder in America

In every country around the world, there is the problem of murder. There are literally thousands of cases of unprovoked murder, but I wish to deal with the subject from the viewpoint of American society.

Society is like a growing vine, never the same – either growing or dying, increasing or decreasing. It will go up or down, depending on the way the people go. Just because our foreparents in America had democracy is no sign that our children will have it.

In every generation democracy must be reborn or it will die. The same is true of Christianity. We could have a Christian society in one generation and a pagan society among the same people in the next generation.

The values and morals of one generation must be born into the next in order for their way of life to be carried on in that society.

I have written this book to point out the conditions that have become a part of our everyday lives. The words will be strong, but they must be.

It is remarkable and amazing to me that in America – the country to which more people seek to migrate than any other nation on the globe – murder is so very prevalent. You cannot pick up a newspaper or a magazine, or listen to a newscast over radio or television, without reading or hearing about it.

In America there are more than 20,000 persons murdered every year. That means one every twenty-six minutes! Half of those die from being shot with a gun.

Unprovoked Murder

Most of these murders are unprovoked and are committed by men and women who have already failed at
rehabilitation programs in our prison houses, in our
penitentiaries, and in our clinics. These murderers are a
burden and a danger to society as a whole.

Our jails and penitentiaries are burdened to capacity
with men and women who have taken human life by the
tens of thousands. Where there should be two prisoners,
there are six.

Our wisest judicial minds are troubled about the
future of these murderers and of the prisons which house
them. Men of law don't know what to do about the situation. They do everything they can to reform the criminal;
but when released, he often returns to crime and many
times to an even worse life.

A Time of Decision

America is now at the point of final decision in this
matter: *What will we do with America's killers today?*

The nation trembles under the burden of this evil.

Millions of people live in abject fear that they will be
next on the criminal's hit list.

Some are afraid to ride a commercial aircraft because
of international gangsterism by hijacking.

Some are afraid to do their shopping – afraid of being
mugged, or robbed, or maybe even murdered, as they
walk across the parking lots of the big malls.

In this country, 20,000 murders a year is altogether too
much. One murder every twenty-six minutes is too much!
We must do something about it.

*Who bears the blame for these wanton murders, both
provoked and unprovoked?*

There are several areas where we could lay the blame,
but I feel that if each of us takes a personal responsibility,
we can resolve the problem. Placing the blame on some-

one else will not bring relief. If we expect to find a solution, you and I must face the problem head-on.

Americans can meet a challenge when they set their hearts to it, and I firmly believe that we can set our hearts to do this.

I Have Witnessed Murder

Having seen murder, I can testify that it is not a pleasant sight.

While in hinterland China, as I was riding down a city street in a ricksha, I saw a man being stoned to death on the sidewalk. I commanded the ricksha man to stop, and with my interpreter I got out to investigate.

Both men and women were throwing stones that were twice the size of a man's hand. Children were laughing.

When I pushed back the crowd, there lying on the ground before me was a Chinese man, battered to pieces. It was a horrible sight.

Working fast, my interpreter asked a few people, "What's going on? Why is a man being killed? What's happening?"

Finally, someone said, "He was caught stealing. He was a thief, so we've killed him."

We waited a few moments as the crowd began to break up. Standing there across the street were some policemen, who had watched the killing take place, but made no attempt to stop it.

The next morning the dead body was hauled away by the garbage men to be burned at the garbage dump.

I may have been the only person so severely hurt that day, excepting the man who died. I could not get over it. I lived with it.

One thought haunted me: *What if that man had not been a thief? What if somebody had lied and screamed, "Thief!" when it wasn't true?*

3

Whether guilty or innocent, that man died without a judge, an attorney, or a trial. He had no help and died there on the sidewalk in that far-inland Asian town.

Another time while near Tibet, I saw a man executed by being tied to a thorn tree. The thorns were unlike those we have in America. They were three or four inches long and ten times stronger than those here. I saw men tie that man to a thorn tree, then kick him into the tree, driving those thorns four or five inches into his body, from his head to his feet.

As blood began to pour from all parts of his body, the man screamed in agony, but they kept kicking him deeper and deeper into the tree.

I could not find out through my interpreter what the man had done wrong. He was being executed, not by police, but by civilians; and no one seemed to know why. That event burned a place in my consciousness that I could not escape.

Murder Without Reason

Today, so many horrible things happen without reason. A member of my church, standing on his own sidewalk, saw a young man riding a motorcycle on fresh asphalt and destroying it.

He said, "Son, you shouldn't do that."

The motorcycle rider came over to him and struck him in the head with his helmet. This man dropped dead in his tracks. His widow was so deeply grieved that she died soon after.

We later discovered that the motorcycle rider was out on parole for another crime.

That happened in my own town. It could have happened in yours or in any town in America.

We Have a Problem

Unprovoked murder: What can we do about it? What *must* we do about it?

Is there a difference between the person who actually kills with a gun and the society that permits this kind of murder to continue?

Is there a difference in the kind of person who dynamites a boat, murdering all on board, as happened to Lord Mountbatten of England and those with him on his yacht?

Is there a difference in those who commit arson – burning a school, or a factory, or a hospital, or a hotel?

Unprovoked murder in any form is a terrible tragedy upon society, revealing a force not normal to humans. It is a netherworld spectra which stalks thousands of unsuspecting people.

What kind of person is it who commits murder or multiple murders?

Are they odd looking?

Are they peculiar in their dress?

Are they strange in their talk?

Just what kind of person would murder other persons?

In the following chapters, I will be discussing unprovoked murder using, as examples, several documented cases of violent crime. The cases we will consider are:

1. The case of **Roland Kashney** in Chicago, charged with two counts of murder; found guilty of one.
2. The case of **John Wayne Gacy** in Chicago, guilty of murdering thirty-three young men and boys.
3. The case of **Richard Benjamin Speck** in Chicago, guilty of murdering eight student nurses.
4. The case of **David Berkowitz, "the Son of Sam,"** in New York City, guilty of murdering six persons.
5. The case of **Theodore Streleski** in Los Angeles,

5

guilty of murdering a Stanford University math professor.

6. The case of **Arne Cheyenne Johnson** in Brookfield, Connecticut, charged with one count of murder.
7. The case of **Stephen Judy** in Indianapolis, found guilty and executed for murdering a mother and her three small children.
8. The case of **Charles Manson** in Los Angeles, charged with murdering actress Sharon Tate and six others.
9. The case of **Jim Jones** in Guyana, South America, in which 900 cult members committed suicide.
10. The case of **Peter Sutcliffe, "the Yorkshire Ripper,"** in London, England, guilty of murdering thirteen women.

2

Ten Cases of Murder

Case No. 1: ROLAND KASHNEY

Two Persons Dead

Roland Kashney was charged with two bludgeon murders: In 1970 a sixty-five-year-old woman was beaten to death with a porcelain toilet seat; in 1975 a fifty-five-year-old man was fatally wounded in his Chicago home from blows with a wrench.

According to police, Kashney confessed to committing two murders, then later withdrew his confession. He claims that the devil made him confess a lie as demons severely beat him.

He says that in fright he had confessed to murders of which he was innocent. Policemen who were present at the time could not see the demons beating him.

After more than five years of incarceration, Richard Kashney was brought to trial.

I was subpoenaed to appear at the Cook County Criminal Court to give "expert witness," as the judge calls it, to what the State's prosecuting attorney termed "empirical powers influencing a human person."

The judge and court chose me as "expert witness" because of the books and articles I have written on the subject of demon possession and my personal experiences in over 100 nations of the world.

It is their considered opinion and that of the defendant, Mr. Kashney, who also requested my appearance

7

at the trial, that there do exist sinister and malevolent entities which are capable of possessing and attacking human beings.

It is unique in the criminal courts of our land to subpoena this type of witness and to hear testimony of netherworld activities found to be satanic and demonic. The judicial and legal authorities are evidently convinced that there are in existence real powers, other than human or divine, which can invade human affairs.

Four Visitors from the State Attorney's Office

Attorneys and certified court reporters asked for and received permission to travel 100 miles to my office in South Bend, Indiana, for an intense briefing on the subject of demons and human possession by spirits.

These four gentlemen – Brian Collins, Jack Smedon, Bob Colby, and Michael Harnet – represented the Prosecuting Attorney on behalf of the State of Illinois against Kashney, the accused.

I assured these four attorneys and assistant attorneys that my appearance at the Circuit Court of Cook County Criminal Division was in behalf of truth as I understood it from the Bible and from personal experiences. I made it clear that as a witness I would not appear in behalf of either the State or the accused.

I pointed out that since these violent crimes are on the increase in our country today, we must seek for an honest and truthful answer to this most serious problem of murder. So many murders today are unprovoked, and most involve the lives of innocent women and children.

It is known by our entire population how multiple murders have been committed in heinous fashion, oftentimes for no apparent reason, since there are no feelings of anger or hate between killer and victim.

Is it possible for a human being to be possessed by an entity beyond human power and strength?

Can a person become possessed by a power outside and beyond himself so that he becomes a destroyer, equipped with ability that is inhuman?

For over two hours these expertly trained, legal-minded men listened to my side of the story.

In our session together, I revealed from the Bible some intricate complexities of demon-inspired transgressions. They received from me considerable written material on the subject, including books and magazines.

Very simply, I stated that to class all of these crimes together with the one word *insanity* is wrong for the accused as well as for the victim.

These attorneys were deeply moved by the interview. They heard things that day like they had never heard before and agreed that there could possibly be strange powers moving behind the facade of humans which the present legal justice may not be adequately acquainted with.

I was to meet them again as I stood before the judge in Cook County Criminal Court. Here is a portion of the testimony I gave at that time:

Q: "Are you familiar with demonology?"

A: "Yes."

Q: "Do you consider yourself an expert in demonology?"

A: "Yes."

Q: "Have you done any exorcisms?"

A: "Yes."

Q: "How many? Where?"

A: "Thousands. South America, Hong Kong, Indonesia, the Philippines. I lived with my family in the Philippines for five years."

Q: "What is your definition of demons?"

9

A: "A demon is an entity. They fell with Lucifer. These spirits seek to have human expression."

Q: "Have you ever seen a demon-possessed person?"

A: "Yes. I have seen many people possessed."

Q: "Have you known people who have seen demons in others?"

A: "Yes. A man with great religious beliefs is able to see this better than anyone else."

Q: "You preach the Bible?"

A: "Yes, I do."

Q: "This possession or manifestation you are talking about – that has to be from external manifestation."

A: "Normally a person can look like anyone else, but can be demon possessed."

Q: "By looking around the courtroom now, could you find someone that is possessed?"

A: "No. A person can change in his total personality . . . such as when a woman's voice goes much deeper than a man's voice."

Q: "In your book, *Demons - The Answer Book* . . . you believe demon spirits are drawn to large cities."

A: "Yes. I believe the demon spirits are more active in the larger cities and are a place of worship of evil."

Q: "When was the first time you met Roland Kashney?"

A: "December 1980."

Q: "When a demon possesses a person, could one person see it and no one else? Are there circumstances when only one person can see it?"

A: "When the Lord Jesus went into a certain place, the person cried out and the Lord set him free. He became different. There is always a manifestation. The Lord Jesus said, 'Go into all the world.' This is the Great Commission. Any Christian

10

should be able to cast demon spirits out of another person. They have to discern it in order to do it."

* * *

Roland Kashney was found not guilty of murdering the woman, not guilty of robbery, but guilty of killing the man. His verdict was to be appealed and his case set for retrial.

Case No. 2: JOHN WAYNE GACY

Thirty-three Boys Murdered

John Wayne Gacy of Des Plaines, Illinois, was pronounced guilty for the murder of thirty-three young men and boys.

When police discovered one of the bodies in a river, tire tracks were found at the scene. Through the work of one hard-working detective, the evidence eventually led to John Gacy.

Police obtained a search warrant and went to Gacy's home. There they found certain items that linked him to one of the latest victims. When confronted with this evidence, Gacy broke down and confessed.

At Gacy's direction, lawmen dug beneath his house and garage to find skeletons and decomposing bodies. In all, a total of twenty-nine bodies were unearthed on Gacy's property, and the bodies of four boys linked with Gacy were discovered in the river.

Double Life of a Clown

John Wayne Gacy was thirty-six years old when taken into custody. The press described him as "chunky, moon-faced, and jovial." He had been most successful at leading a double life.

Gacy was a local businessman, a contractor. He lived in a nice house and was accepted by friends and neighbors. As a member and promoter of the local Democratic Party, Gacy was described as "always there," willing to do the jobs nobody else wanted to do.

Gacy very often dressed in a clown's suit for festive occasions in the community. Billing himself as "Pogo the Clown," he would perform magic tricks for children.

To the eye, John Wayne Gacy appeared to be an upstanding citizen. He was a business and social success; yet all the while, he was destroying human lives. He was indicted for murdering more people than any other person in United States history.

The citizens of the Chicago suburb wonder why it took the police three years to discover the man who had killed thirty-three youths and buried twenty-six of them in the forty-nine-foot crawl space under his house.

No doubt Gacy thought that by donning the clown's suit, by being an active worker in the local Democratic Party, even posing with a Chicago mayor, he would be able to hide his true self and escape detection.

You may ask, "How could he get control over all these young men and boys?"

By using his clown tricks.

He would invite them to his home to offer them a job and then begin showing them tricks. First, he would put handcuffs on his wrists and maneuver out of them. Then he would volunteer to teach them how to do it. Once handcuffed, they were his prisoners. He forced them to engage in deviate sex with him, then choked them to death.

"Something" Made Him Kill

Gacy took these boys into his friendship only to have them die at his hand, in his home, and be buried beneath his house.

Why would a man kill thirty-three young people?
He had no quarrel with them.
He hardly knew them.
He had no reason for doing it, except that "something" within him gave him a strange compulsion to hurt and destroy.

Gacy's two defense attorneys argued that their client was innocent by reason of insanity. In his closing statement, one attorney sought to create sympathy for the defendant by quoting from Robert Louis Stevenson's, *The Strange Case of Dr. Jekyll and Mr. Hyde.*

Throughout his thirty-day trial, Gacy held to his confession. He remained stone-faced as the relatives of his victims sat sobbing only a few feet away.

Though a line of 101 witnesses had marched across the courtroom to the witness chair, it took only one hour and fifty minutes for the jury to reach their verdict. Gacy was found guilty.

The next day the judge pronounced Gacy's sentence: death by electrocution. Under Illinois law, he was given an automatic appeal.

The day the court clerk read the names of the victims and pronounced the guilty verdict, Gacy addressed his attorneys: "Cheer up, boys, and keep a straight face." The news media said that on his way out of the courtroom Gacy winked at a sheriff's deputy.

Case No. 3: RICHARD BENJAMIN SPECK

Eight Student Nurses Murdered

On the night of July 13, an intruder carrying a knife and a gun, entered a nurses' apartment building in southeast Chicago.

At gunpoint, the intruder gathered together nine nurses into a bedroom and bound them. Then slowly he led eight of them one by one to other parts of the house where he murdered them by cutting, stabbing, and strangling them.

The remarkable thing is how none of the nurses cried out for help. How could eight young women be overwhelmed by only one man? One policeman speculated that they could have been totally paralyzed by fear like a bird is before a cobra.

Without a cry, without trying to escape, they died – all except one. A twenty-three-year-old Filipino nurse, Corazon Amurao, slid under a bunk and was apparently overlooked by the killer. She stayed there until the next morning – until she was sure he was gone.

Matching fingerprints found in the nurses' home, Chicago police sought for Richard Benjamin Speck, a twenty-four-year-old drifter from Dallas, Texas. He was positively identified twenty-eight hours after the mutilated bodies were discovered.

When Speck heard that the police were searching for him, he tried to commit suicide by cutting his arms. He was taken into custody while in a hospital, suffering from the wounds.

Here we have a man who destroyed eight women. Why?

Speck told the doctors of his drug abuse and addiction. He related his violent fightings and wild drinking. He said he remembered taking barbiturates and drinking alcohol with a group of sailors the night of the dormitory massacre. That was his last memory before waking up the next morning with a gun and wondering where he got it.

The surviving nurse identified Speck as the killer. Though he accepted her accusation, he insisted he remembered nothing.

Symbols of Death

Speck's arm is a mass of tattoos. He said most of them were put on when he would go with a group of Navy buddies to the tattooer.

One of the tattoos below his right elbow is a long dagger with a snake coiled around it. On the little finger of his right hand is a solitary letter, L. Above his left elbow is a grinning skull with the words, "Born to Raise Hell."

While being questioned by a psychologist, Speck rolled up his trouser leg and revealed an obscene picture tattooed on his shin.

Tattoos cannot be removed, so Speck carried those symbols of death on his body at all times. He couldn't get away from them.

Fits of Anger

The judge appointed a public defender as defense counsel for Speck, and a court hearing was set for early November. From July to October, an examining panel of psychologists worked to prepare the report on Speck, regarding the eight murdered nurses.

During this time of examination, Speck told one of the five psychologists, "You see, when I'm sober, I'm . . . I'm . . . well . . . okay. But when I drink . . . I'll tell you, once I smashed my hand through a wall rather than to hit her."

The psychologist stated that Speck's hatred for his stepfather and for his former wife were two of the greatest hatreds of his life.

He confessed that once, in a fit of anger, he kicked his mother in the head, seriously injuring her.

Later, in one of his more relaxed moments, he said, "I should have seen a doctor when I was eighteen years old, when I beat the hell out of my mother."

The psychologist asked what was happening inside him when he kicked his own mother and if he was sorry. Unemotionally, Speck replied, "Nope," and showed no interest in pursuing the subject.

About the Nurses

The psychologist talked long hours with Speck, discussing his feelings about the eight murders and his fits of anger.

Speck asked, "Could this mean I can't control myself when I'm angry and wild, not knowing what I'm doing?"

In his most serious moment, he declared, "I don't know why I killed them."

He said that he had not been to the nurses' dormitory before and did not know anything about it or the nurses. He just went there and did it.

The doctor asked, "Do you ever think about that at night?"

He replied, "Naw, it's all gone. I only think about it when people ask me questions."

Of the eight student nurses Speck was accused of murdering, only one, Gloria Davy, was also sexually assaulted.

Savage Impulses

Speck very often acted out of savage impulses. While in prison, he did such things as assault a fellow prisoner and throw hot water on the sergeant on duty.

A most dramatic moment in prison came as one of the psychologists was talking with Speck in his cell. Suddenly, Speck leaned toward the doctor as a razor blade flashed between his fingers.

Holding the blade only inches from the doctor's face, he said, "Look, if I'm such a killer, how come I don't kill you? I have nothing to lose."

Then he put the razor blade back in his pocket and smiled.

The Verdict

It took the jury only forty-nine minutes to reach a unanimous decision. Their verdict: "We, the jury, find the defendant, Richard Benjamin Speck, guilty of murder in the manner and form as charged in the Indictment, and we fix his punishment at death."

Of the death penalty, Speck declared to his medical counsel, "I want it to be. I want it over with. I'm ready for the chair."

Once when he heard about a mass murder in Arizona, he told his doctor: "I would like to take care of him. My last wish is to kill him, just kill him, and I will die happy."

Case No. 4: DAVID BERKOWITZ
"Son of Sam"

Six Persons Dead

At the time of his incarceration at age twenty-five, David Berkowitz was known to America as "the Son of Sam" killer. Using a .44 caliber pistol, "the Son of Sam" was responsible for an orgy of murder that put metropolitan New York in a state of terror for a year. In all, his murder spree left six victims dead and seven wounded.

Guilty as Charged

David Berkowitz declared himself guilty of all charges against the protests of his attorneys who desired for him to be found not guilty by reason of insanity.[1]

---

[1]*Time Magazine,* May 22, 1978.

Born Richard David Falco and given up at birth by his unwed mother, David was later adopted by Nathan Berkowitz, the owner of a small hardware store in the Bronx, New York.

David was a quiet child. A sharp contrast in personality was displayed later in life when he called himself "the Son of Sam" and signed himself "the Master of Reality."

In the Army, Berkowitz served in Korea as a rifleman in the Second Infantry Division. It was while stationed in Korea that he plunged into drugs, including LSD.

The sparsely furnished apartment in Yonkers where he lived was located on the seventh floor of a building that overlooked the Hudson River. Police found that the windows were covered by sheets to keep neighbors from seeing in. Pornographic magazines were scattered around on the floor.

An Instrument of the Devil

After his incarceration, Berkowitz gave details of his murderous activities. Describing himself as "an instrument of the devil," he told of hearing strange voices which commanded him to kill. He said these voices gave him power to act beyond his will or responsibility.

He receives these orders to kill from a dog, a black Labrador retriever. However, he went on to explain that the message actually came from a 6,000-year-old demon who was reincarnated as his next-door neighbor.

In addition to his rash of killing, Berkowitz also kept a diary in which were listed 1,400 fires he had set in New York City.

Here was a man who committed heinous acts of destruction through a direct relationship with demon power.

During that terrifying year, Berkowitz called himself by several names: Duke of Death; Wicked King Wicker;

Twenty-two Disciples of Hell; and John Wheaties, Rapist and Suffocator of Young Girls.

How He Killed

The "Son of Sam" did not look for any particular kind of girl. When he got "a calling," he would cruise certain neighborhoods in his Ford Galaxie sedan and look for a spot.

In choosing his victims, Berkowitz admitted favoring girls from Queens because they were the prettiest. His first victim was only eighteen years of age.

The officers who interviewed Berkowitz said he had no remorse for the killings, that to him it was the same as eating an ice cream cone. Psychologists described him neurotic, schizophrenic, paranoid, and psychopathic.[2]

The night David Berkowitz was taken into custody by the police, he was carrying a semi-automatic rifle in his car.

He told the police he had planned to drive out to a fashionable Hampton resort in Long Island and shoot into a discotheque or nightclub.

He wanted to kill.

With a smile, he said he was ready to go down in a blaze of glory.

Case No. 5: THEODORE STRELESKI

Brutal Murder of College Professor

Theodore Streleski was the perfect image of a mathematics professor: tall and bony, with stringy brown hair and an unkempt beard, flecked with gray.

---

[2]*Time Magazine*, August 22, 1977.

But Theodore Streleski possessed a spirit of hate and revenge that was beyond human realization, beyond the way a human normally thinks or talks.

Streleski's Reason for Murder

Because he was not developing in life as he desired, Streleski vented his feelings of anger on a fellow professor, Karel De Leeuw.

When the court asked Streleski if he murdered the Stanford mathematics department head, he replied simply, "Yes."

"Why did you kill the mathematics professor?"

"So that the State of California may provide sustenance for me to study my math."

"Do you feel that this is morally correct?"

"Yes."

Though a very competent person mentally, Streleski's problem was with finances. He hated having to do menial jobs – tasks that he considered beneath his ability.

As he explained to police: "I didn't want to be involved in making a living or any struggle situation. I felt it was more constructive for me to commit a murder than to hunt for a job. I now have what I want: the leisure to study without the distraction of having to support myself. I view prison as a sort of utopia with some restraints."

Countdown to Murder

Theodore Streleski entered the University of Illinois at the age of sixteen. In less than three years, he finished his work in engineering physics. His ambition was to be a mathematician, so he moved to California to earn a Ph.D. in math from Stanford University.

During his time at Stanford, Streleski's advisor and professor was Karel De Leeuw. After deciding that the professor was blocking his progress, Streleski began living a countdown.

For three years he wanted to kill De Leeuw, but he deliberately waited until his thesis was acceptable. He felt obligated to complete his thesis for his own self-respect and to prove to others that his murder was not because of sour grapes.

Of the professor, Streleski said, "Dr. De Leeuw helped to take nineteen years of my life." He said he just could not let that pass, so he killed him.

He struck the professor four times on the head with a two-pound sledge hammer which he carried in a red flight bag. Then he placed a plastic bag over the victim's head because, as he said, he did not want to offend the person who found the body.

No Feelings of Remorse

Streleski decided to turn himself in at a time of day when there would be the least commotion, so he picked the predawn hours. While waiting for that time to come, he read a Western novel.

It was 3:30 a.m. on August 19 when Theodore Streleski entered the North County Jail and told deputies: "I hit him in the head with a hammer. It's in the bag over there near the door. There's some blood on it. It's in the plastic bag."

Streleski showed no remorse for his deed. Given similar circumstances, he said he would do it again.

He even had a second choice as a murder victim: Professor David Gilbarg, chairman of the physics department. Streleski said he attended a two-year seminar with Professor Gilbarg in which the professor sneered at him.

When questioned, Gilbarg said he had never taught a two-year seminar and did not remember Streleski in any of his shorter seminars.

The Murder Sentence

The attorney for the defense argued that his client suffered from "diminished mental capacity."

Streleski was not sentenced for first degree murder, but for second degree. With good behavior, he would be eligible for parole within six years!

Case No. 6: ARNE CHEYENNE JOHNSON

One Man Dead

Arne Cheyenne Johnson – a slender, muscular youth of nineteen years with curly blond hair – killed his friend, Alan Bono, the manager of a dog kennel. This was the first slaying in history in the small town of Brookfield, Connecticut.

Did the devil make Arnie Johnson kill?

His defense attorney, Marvin Minnella, is working with psychic experts and Catholic priests, seeking to prove that the devil is responsible. Minnella says he has substantial evidence to prove that what occurred was a result of demonic possession. The story, he says, is more frightening than "The Exorcist."

According to the Associated Press, this bizarre story began eight months prior to the killing when Arne Johnson was in the presence of some priests as they sought to rid a twelve-year-old boy, David Glatzel, of demons.

Tape recordings made at the time reveal the boy making guttural and hissing sounds, cursing his mother, threatening to kill those present in the room, and even using supernatural strength at times to resist them.

Observing the conditions of the boy, Johnson became angry. He dared the devil to leave the boy alone and try him instead. It was something like a challenge to fight.

He screamed at the devil, "Take me on! Leave him and take me on!"

Though Johnson was unconverted and knew nothing of the born-again experience, he felt that he was stronger than the devil. The priests, present at the time, were astonished when the young man ordered the devil to take him on.

For the next several months, young Johnson had several strange manifestations, encountering what came to be known as "the beast." He would growl, his eyes would roll, and he would jerk uncontrollably. One day, while in church, he started stomping his feet. He stood up, shouting and cursing, and had to be dragged out of church.

Then one night Johnson suddenly stabbed to death his friend, Alan Bono.

At the exact time of the murder twelve-year-old David woke from a deep sleep, screaming. He began to describe what was happening with Arne as if he were there. David said "the beast" forced Arne to kill.

Regarding the killing, Johnson said he didn't remember being in Bono's apartment and didn't realize he had done it.

Johnson was charged with murder and placed in jail under a $125,000 bond. His friends say he was charged with murdering a man that he liked.

His attorneys used demon possession as a defense, arguing that "the devil made Mr. Johnson do it."

Attorney Minnella says in strong words, "The courts, I imagine, have dealt with the existence of God. Now they are going to have to deal with the existence of the devil. People may not believe in the devil, but he exists."

Case No. 7: STEPHEN JUDY

Four Persons Dead

Stephen Judy, a former construction worker, raped and strangled Terry Chasteen, a young mother; then drowned her three children: Misty Ann, age 5; Stephen Michael, age 4; and Mark Lewis, age 2.

Judy had a long criminal record that began at age thirteen when he raped and brutally stabbed a woman. Eight of his last eleven years were spent in and out of prison and mental institutions for rape, robbery, and burglary.

Death Penalty

After receiving the death penalty for the murder of the young mother and her three children, Judy requested that the penalty be carried out.

He actually threatened the jury by telling them how to deliver his sentence: "You better vote for the death penalty, or it might be you or one of your family next."

Judy recognized another power or spirit over him.

At a news conference, he told reporters that he did not lose any sleep over the slayings of these four people. To him, it was just something that happened.

He told the press that the death penalty was fair punishment for the crimes he had committed and felt that it should be carried out. He said he did not believe in God; but he did believe in reincarnation, though he didn't know exactly how.

Stephen Judy of Indianapolis, Indiana, was twenty-four years of age when the 2,822 volts of electricity pulsed through his body. He was the first person to be executed in Indiana in twenty years.

In his last talk with his foster mother, Judy said, "Don't

24

make me a headstone. Just drive a wooden stake into the ground."

After the execution, Indiana Governor Robert Orr made this statement: "Now that this difficult ordeal is over with, I am at peace with myself because I believe justice has prevailed."

The case of Stephen Judy would have to involve a form of demonic possession. It is not normal for a human to murder a mother without reason, then kill her three small children.

Case No. 8: CHARLES MANSON

Seven Persons Dead

One of the most notorious cases in American history is known as "the Manson Case" and has been termed the most senseless crime of the century.

It was Charles Manson who screamed at his hippie followers: "Society has wronged me. I will kill whatever pigs are in that house. Go in there and get them!"

His bewitched and bewildered followers, dressed in black, broke into a secluded mansion in Benedict Canyon, California. Their orgy of hacking, stabbing, and shooting left five persons dead, including actress Sharon Tate, who was twenty-six years of age and eight months pregnant.

The night following the Tate murders, the "family," as they called themselves, killed a middle-aged couple, Mr. and Mrs. Leon La Bianca, at their home in the Los Feliz area.

All of the victims were strangers to Manson and his clan.

The story goes that Sharon Tate had rented the house from Terry Melcher, Doris Day's son. Apparently, Manson had a grudge against Melcher for refusing to hear a song he had written. Manson ordered everyone in the house killed, not knowing who the tenants were.

To show how senseless it was, one victim – Steven Parent, eighteen years of age – was simply visiting the caretaker's cottage at the time.

According to "family" member Susan Atkins, they picked the La Bianca couple at random and murdered them just to prove they hadn't lost their nerve.

History of Crime

Charles Manson had a five-page criminal record. As the son of a teenage prostitute, he never knew his father. While his prostitute mother was often in jail, young Manson was shifted from relatives to foster parents to reformatories.

His young life was one of rejection and delinquency. His last and most permanent home proved to be the Indiana Boys' School where he was taken at age fourteen.

At age twenty, Manson decided to go to California, so he stole a car and struck out for Los Angeles.

For the next several years, Manson drifted in and out of jail. While in prison, he became interested in music. He learned to play the guitar and decided he was a composer.

Another area of special interest to him was the occult. He spent time reading the Bible and studying about Scientology. Soon he decided that the Book of Revelation had predicted the Beatles.

When released from prison in 1967, Manson traveled to Haight-Ashbury in San Francisco. The next year he gathered together a group of misfits, moved to Los Angeles, and finally settled on the Spahn Movie Ranch. From there, he made his attacks upon society.

When police raided the ranch and discovered stolen goods, Manson led his followers into Death Valley. There, in an almost savage existence, they lived by stealing cars for cash and sometimes eating garbage.

A Cult in Action

The Manson "family" could be called a semi-religious hippie cult. Susan Atkins said it was led by a bearded person named Mahdi, who dispatched the girl killers with hunting knives to commit at least eight murders. According to Miss Atkins, they often styled themselves as slaves to their leader.

The national news media reported of suspicions that the group was amusing itself with black magic rites and drugs. One man who practiced a native Jamaican voodoo was a friend to the group. This may be the reason why, at the Tate murder site, a hood was found over the head of victim Jay Sebring and a rope was binding him to Miss Tate.

Charles Manson held a strange and cultish spell over all his followers. Mesmerized and hypnotized, they obeyed him like God. His female followers called him God and Satan. Some of them believed he was the Messiah come again.

Manson read deeply in Oriental theology and believed in reincarnation. He did not accept the significance of an individual and would say, "Let's shoot and kill all of the pigs. They are destroying the earth."

Charles Manson possessed a tremendous amount of hostility and anger toward all mankind. To have the girls who lived with him do the killing was his way of expressing hatred for the total society.

The Trial

During his trial, Manson pulled some strange antics. One time he actually vaulted over the defense table and tried to attack the judge with a sharpened pencil. Another time he swung several blows at his defense attorney and had to be pulled away by the bailiff.

Manson appeared in the Los Angeles courtroom wearing on his forehead what he called a "symbol of apartness": an "X" in his own dried blood. As he said, "I have X-ed myself from your world."

Manson's trial proved to be the longest murder trial in California history – 129 days. He refused to plead insanity and was found guilty of first degree murder.

Case No. 9: JIM JONES

Nine Hundred People Dead

Jim Jones was a self-proclaimed messiah who mesmerized his followers, giving them the impression that he was omniscient. By demanding total loyalty and adoration from them, Jones was able to lead his community of 900 people in Guyana, South America, in a ritual of mass suicide.

His Beginning

James Warren Jones was born in 1931 in Lynn, Indiana, but his story really began with the spiritist activities of his mother. Torn between the choice of a career or marriage, she dreamed repeatedly of her dead mother. Then one day her mother called to her from beyond the grave and said she would bear a son who would right the wrongs of the world.

Jones' mother accepted a proposal of marriage and, when her first child was a boy, she was convinced that he was a messiah.

Raised a Methodist, Jim Jones was fascinated by

pulpit oratory. As a young child, his favorite game was playing "pretend church."

His Career as Pastor

In his twenties, Jones became pastor of a Methodist church in Indianapolis, but his liberalist ideas about church integration caused problems in the community. Soon disenchanted with the Methodist church, Jones began his own church and eventually opened the first Peoples Temple.

After a visit with Father Divine, the famous black cult leader in Philadelphia, Jones adopted Divine's idea of insisting on fierce personal loyalty from his church members. He set up a committee in the church to question anyone who dared to speak against him.

Warped Theology

It wasn't long before Jones' view of his own worth was utmost in his thinking. In his sermons he declared that he no longer believed in the Virgin Birth. At times he would throw his Bible on the floor, exclaiming, "Too many people are looking at this, instead of at me!"

In 1962 Jones moved his family to Brazil. There his messianic ideas grew stronger and he began doing good deeds for the poverty-stricken people. It was while here that Jones visited Guyana and apparently caught a glimpse of a remote utopian settlement.

When he returned home, Jones seemed even more caught up with his own "calling." Money had become high in his thinking, and people were welcome at the church if they had money to donate.

Though Jones wasn't a Christian, the concept of Christianity was very much with him. He began telling friends that he himself was Jesus Christ. Suddenly, he was willing to do whatever was necessary to win the people to his side. Fake "healings" became important tools of his trade.

Warped sexual practices were also a part of Jones' lifestyle. He engaged in sexual activities with his followers – both male and female.

Jones considered himself to be the only meaningful source of guidance, discipline, and sex for his followers. He required everyone in the cult to refer to him as "Father."

A Suicidal Ending

When threatened by newspaper investigations that would expose his activities, Jones moved his people to Guyana where he had leased a 27,000-acre tract of land.

As investigators drew closer and exposure seemed certain, Jones devised a way that he and his followers could perform what he called "a dignified revolutionary act."

This "act" was mass suicide.

Vats of cyanide were brought from the medical shack, and one by one the Peoples Temple followers took the poison and died.

In the midst of children wailing and mothers crying, Jim Jones joined the ritual by putting a bullet through his head.

Case No. 10: PETER SUTCLIFFE
"The Yorkshire Ripper"
Thirteen Women Dead

In October 1975, the mutilated body of a twenty-eight year-old prostitute was found in Leeds, a community in the Yorkshire area of England. Five years, seventeen attacks, and thirteen gruesome murders later, police were still searching for what they termed "the murderer without a motive." Soon, he was being referred to as a "modern-day Jack the Ripper."

The first few victims had been prostitutes; others were respectable young women. The last, number thirteen, was a twenty-year-old university student, described as quiet and respectable – a perfect example of the girl next door.

After the eleventh killing, the assistant chief constable of West Yorkshire was quoted as saying, "Clearly, we have a homicidal maniac at large."

In June of one year the Yorkshire police received a 260-word tape recording from "Jack the Ripper," telling of plans to strike again that year: "Maybe September or October – even sooner if I get the chance." The next killing, number twelve, occurred in September.

Psychiatrists' Explanation

Over the five-year period, there were as much as thirteen and fourteen months between killings. Why such long gaps? Police have no explanation.

According to one psychiatrist, there is no accurate explanation for crimes such as this. He admits, "Nobody really knows what makes a man do this. Is it innate evil? Did his mother leave him? We just don't know."

Psychiatric experts describe murderers like "Jack" as being "over-controlled psychopaths."

They explain that an "over-controlled" man is capable of keeping himself under control emotionally until he reaches a certain point. He seems quiet until pressures within him mount. When he reaches that "point," he must strike out.

The extent to which this "quiet type" of murderer vents

his anger and aggression will tend to be much greater and his crimes are always the most vicious.[1]

Confession

A few weeks after the body of victim number thirteen was discovered, police made an arrest. Peter Sutcliffe, age thirty-five, was arrested initially for petty theft, then formally charged with one count of murder for the death of the thirteenth victim.

Sutcliffe, described as a quiet, hard-working truck driver, eventually confessed and was found guilty of committing the murders.

* * *

Kashney, Gacy, Speck, Berkowitz, Streleski, Johnson, Judy, Manson, Jim Jones, Sutcliffe – all are human beings.

All were born into the world as innocent babies.

But as they grew up in our society, something happened.

They changed.

They became strange, evil, possessed – and the result was unprovoked murder.

---

[1]*Esquire*, January 1981, "The Ripper" by Guy Martin, pp. 60,61.

3
Why Does a Human Murder Humans?

The problem of murder is not new. It has been around for a very long time, beginning with the first family on the face of the earth. God's first man and woman, Adam and Eve, bore two sons, Cain and Abel. Cain was a murderer; he killed his brother Abel.

The Book of Job is said to be the first book of the Bible ever written. Perhaps it is the oldest book in the world. Job 24:14 says, *The murderer rising with the light killeth the poor and needy, and in the night is as a thief.*

If the oldest book known among men makes a statement like this, then apparently the subject has been under discussion for quite a while.

Murder is not a new sin; it is not a new problem. It is only an aggravated problem, an enormously growing and increasing problem, one that must be faced head-on.

The Lord Jesus said in Matthew 19:18, *Thou shalt do no murder.* During His three years of ministry on earth, the Lord Jesus Christ reiterated nine of the Ten Commandments. He put them back into focus again and caused man to know that he was responsible under the New Covenant of grace, just as he was under the Old Covenant of the Law.

One of the Ten Commandments states: *Thou shalt not kill* (Exodus 20:13). We must learn *why* we are not to kill.

Why does one person murder another person?

Why does one man desire to destroy the life of another man?

This could perhaps be man's oldest problem.

It could be the deepest problem of medical science today.

It certainly is one of the greatest problems facing modern society as a whole.

In the great judicial world, millions of dollars are being spent as legal experts seek to know how to reform a murderer. The penal institutions have not resolved the problem: What are we to do with him? Where are we to put him?

Psychologists and psychiatrists spend their lives seeking to know why humans act certain ways, why they say and do certain things.

Unprovoked murder, especially multiple murder, is one of the deepest mysteries of what truly motivates a person.

God vs. the Devil

Actually, there are only two motivational powers in our universe: God and the devil.

The motivation of God is the good motivation – the motivation of love. God is a Creator; He is not a destroyer. The Bible says that God is love. (1 John 4:8.)

The other motivation comes from sin and rebellion which, in turn, comes from the devil. The devil was originally in heaven as an archangel, Lucifer, who rebelled against God and was cast out of heaven.

Rebellion and Murder

The motivation of sin and rebellion is the motivation of hate and of destruction.

Rebellion and murder go together. Rebellion will eventually end in murder. There will be no murder without first having rebellion. The Bible says of the devil that he was a murderer from the beginning. (John 8:44.)

Why Does a Human Murder Humans?

From the beginning, man was made in the image and likeness of God. When created, he was given priority on the face of the earth. The very first chapter of the Bible tells how God gave man dominion. Man is the king and the lovely creature he lives with, his woman, is a princess, a queen. (Genesis 1:26,27.)

Commandment To Love

The essence of the Jehovah God is love. All love comes from God. He demonstrates His love through every aspect of His divine personality.

Whenever you find a manifestation of good which can be related to love, you are seeing God because God is love. On the other hand, when you have a manifestation of hate and destruction, you are seeing the evil one, the devil.

In Mark 12:29-31, the Lord Jesus said there are two great commandments, two above all others:

The first of all the commandments is . . . And thou shalt love the Lord thy God with all thy heart, and with all thy soul, and with all thy mind, and with all thy strength: this is the first commandment.

And the second is like, namely this, Thou shalt love thy neighbour as thyself. There is none other commandment greater than these.

The first of these two commandments is the easy one. It is easy to love the One Who loves you, Who cares for you, Who blesses you.

The second commandment takes a little more effort. You are to love your neighbor as yourself. How do you love yourself? You feed and clothe your body. You take good care of yourself. Jesus said you must treat your neighbor the same way.

Upon these two commandments hang the whole of the divine concept of Scripture. If these two are in focus, everything else will be in focus. If you love God and your fellow man, you will know God's love in its fullness.

Love does not destroy; it is not a destroyer.

Love does not kill; it is not a killer.

Love has a deep respect for itself and for others. When you love horses, you won't mistreat them. When you love flowers, you will care for them and be very particular to see that they grow properly.

That which we love, we care for.

There should be one love above all others in this earthly realm: love for the immortal man.

Every human who is born into this world, the Bible says, will live forever. There is no reincarnation – no beginning, and beginning, and beginning again. Every human being lives only one time: forever. The Bible specifically says it is appointed unto man once to die. (Hebrews 9:27.) *Once* – not two, or three, or six, or a million times. That totally eliminates the theory of reincarnation. The Bible very plainly says there is no coming back.

Love knows that human life is immortal, that it will exist forever. When you get love in your heart, then you will know it, too.

Love knows that human life is very precious. The Lord Jesus said that one person is worth more than this whole world. God puts a premium on human life. We must learn to do the same.

The Reason for Murder

Why does one person murder another person?

Simply because he is connected to the wrong power-house.

When a person is connected to God, he will not hurt others. God loves, so he will love. But when he is connected to Satan, he is open to the demonic entities and negative forces in our universe of which Satan is the head. When he is connected to Satan, he is connected to the source of murder.

When a person refuses to respect human life, when he ignores the preciousness of that life, when he determines to destroy the one that God has created in His image and in His likeness, **there is a price to pay** and he must expect to pay it.

When one person destroys another person, he is striking out at God. He is taking it upon himself to remove the force of life from that other person.

A Price for Murder

All of us must realize from the beginning of our lives that there is a price to pay for our deeds. Every person should be taught from the cradle that there is a penalty for taking another life. He should be carefully instructed in the wages of transgression.

In some countries, especially the Arab countries, if a person is caught stealing, his hand is cut off. To their way of thinking, the solution is very simple: If you don't have a hand, you can't steal. But the real problem of theft is not the hand. The real problem comes from within. Their solution never reaches the source of the problem.

Surrounded by Evil

Many of our homes today are destroyed because of anger and hatred. In many instances, they have become breeding places for these evil forces that will eventually culminate in murder.

So many families today never read the Bible and never have a time of family prayer, which is so very important. Because parents were never taught the principles of love, they don't teach their children. They were not taught love and respect, so they don't know how to show love and respect toward others.

The American schools could very well be termed as seedbeds for producing murders. Our school system glibly teaches that man is an animal, just a little higher than the beasts. This removes any recognition of the sacredness of human life.

When a child leaves school, he comes under the influence of movies and television, where he learns how to applaud killers and praise murderers. From the time a child enters kindergarten until he graduates from high school, it is estimated that he has seen a minimum of 18,000 murders on television and in the movies.

What a difference it would make in his personality if he could see 18,000 people being loved, blessed, cared for, healed, and saved!

The Value of Human Life

One of the fastest growing elements in our society is humanism – a philosophy that has infiltrated our entire educational system. This teaches that man does not need a personal God; that because there is no God, man must impulsively do what *he* thinks is right in every circumstance.

In a humanistic society, there are no rules and no laws to govern man's activities. He is his own god and his own savior. The doctrines of humanism totally relieve man of his responsibility to God and to his fellowman.

One of the greatest jobs for our generation is to teach children and adults the preciousness of human life. Beyond doubt, human life is the greatest treasure this world has ever had or ever will have.

Human life is a mystery – from the time of its conception to the time of its departure from the body.

Human life is very beautiful.

Every person can contribute in making this world a better place in which to live.

It Begins in the Home

When proper punishment for misdeeds is given – first in the home, then in the schools – we will be able to save our nation from the sadness and horror of murder, which it is experiencing right at this moment.

We will never be able to do it through legislation or through the judicial system. It must come through our homes and in our schools.

My mother taught me as a little child that I was not to bite other children. She said, "Lester, whenever you bite a child, I will bite you."

And she did!

I screamed and looked at the place on my hand where she had bitten me.

She said, "Now you know how that child feels, so never do it again!"

I was taught from a baby that I had no right to hurt others.

All of us must realize the fact that when one human being takes the life of another, he will be held accountable, not only by the government, but by the God of this universe.

4
Is Unprovoked Murder Insanity?

The word *insanity,* used so flippantly today, comes to us from the Latin word *insanus.* In its origin this word has to do with being feebleminded and mentally ill – not sick in your stomach, but sick in your mind. It has to do with mental derangement, with unsoundness of mind, with lunacy.

The term *insanity* concludes that a person's mind is not flowing precisely and correctly into the details of life and into the problems facing him. Such a person is not normal: He neither thinks nor acts normally. He is incapable of carrying on the ordinary and regular functions of life.

Insanity describes a human mind as having been either destroyed materially and physically, or having been taken over by an ulterior power – a power that functions from outside the person's will.

Temporary Insanity

For several years the criminal courts of the United States have used the phrase, *temporary insanity,* for the purpose of setting free people who have committed terrible and dreadful deeds upon society.

Is *temporary insanity* a true and honest phrase to use in these cases?

The disturbing fact regarding this is that, by using the term *temporary insanity,* the courts in our land have released back into society dangerous men and women. These criminal elements are first sent to hospitals or

41

clinics for observation, then are set free to once again steal, kill, and destroy.

Is unprovoked murder *insanity*?

Is *temporary insanity* a correct verdict in such cases?

Consider the murder cases set out in chapter 2. The men involved were capable of carrying on regular activities. They could drive an automobile, write letters, and converse normally with friends or relatives. Yet beneath all that, there was a desire to kill and destroy human lives.

To the judges and legal authorities of our land, I would like to direct this question: Is it honest to term a person *insane* in order to relieve him of the responsibility of killing a fellow human being when, in fact, that person was capable of carrying on all the normal, natural functions of society? He was the same as any other person except for the fact that he had a desire to kill, whether for a moment or for a period of time.

Why do psychiatrists consider a person to be insane at the time of a murder and legally pronounce him "innocent by reason of *temporary* insanity"?

By doing so, a murderer is legally returned to society.

On their court reports, judges and legal physicians declare that such a person suffers a severe mental illness (schizophrenic paranoia), and they recommend for him what is called "involuntary hospitalization."

With this decision the criminal is placed in an institution which is supported by taxpayers such as you and me. After a period of time, a psychiatrist submits a written report, telling how the prisoner has done a good job while under his care and has shown himself capable of returning to society.

Many times criminals in situations like this are released, only to be taken into custody again after committing the same kind of crime.

Three Elements for Murder

Personally, I believe that unprovoked murder as a whole is not a product of insanity, but can be the result of three elements: anger, jealousy, and demonic activity.

Uncontrolled Anger

If a child is not taught at a very early age to control his anger, he may at some time in his life destroy another person in a fit of rage. When I was a child, anger was not permitted in our home. If I tried to throw a temper tantrum, my mother would throw water on me!

Anger does not always have to be focused directly on another person. You can be angry at God, or angry with society, or angry with people in public positions of authority. Yet you will vent that pent-up anger by striking out at another human being.

Uncontrolled anger can cause murder. A doctor may call it "temporary insanity," but it is not. It is a person permitting himself to be controlled by the devil in fits of anger.

Deep-Rooted Jealousy

Murder can be, and has been, caused by deep-rooted jealousy. Jealousy is a force that can grow in a person and become rooted so deeply within him that it becomes unreal. The Bible says *jealousy is cruel as the grave* (Song of Solomon 8:6). That means it is a killer!

Many times jealousy has absolutely no relationship whatsoever to reality. It comes into a person's consciousness only because that person permits it.

Jealousy, like anger, comes from the devil. It is a part of the devil's arsenal, but the courts will not admit such a thing.

The people who kill out of jealousy are pronounced

"temporarily insane" by the courts; but they do not fit the definition of *insanity*.

Again, I refer to the Latin root of the word *insanity* which means "feeblemindedness." People who kill because of jealousy are not feebleminded. Many times they are lawyers, doctors, and other highly skilled people.

It is dishonest to declare a man insane because he gave himself over to uncontrolled anger or uncontrolled jealousy to the extent that he eventually rose up and killed another person. He is not insane. Jealousy is not insanity!

Jealousy has never solved any problems; it only leads to more. Because of jealousy, a person will take another person's life when he has absolutely no right to do so.

Demon Possession

By demon possession, I mean a person under the influence and direction of a demonic entity. A person can deliberately permit himself to become so full of destruction that he obeys a satanic voice to take a human life.

The devil says, *Strike!* So he strikes.

In some of the cases of unprovoked murder we examined in chapter 2, the murderer claimed that he was told to kill by another "personality." This "personality" was a demonic spirit.

In the Arne Johnson case, young Johnson said he was following the instructions of a being he called "the beast."

David Berkowitz, "the Son of Sam" killer, claimed he was given instructions through a dog. The dog, he said, was controlled by a 6,000-year-old demon.

There are some issues today that our courts deal with, and one of them is the reality of demon possession. Why should we be so sophisticated in this nation and so humanistic that we say a person cannot be under the power of demons?

Is Unprovoked Murder Insanity?

When a man feels the urge to kill so much within himself that he finds a spot and waits for just the right girl to come along, then that man must be dealt with.

We can no longer "solve" a case by dropping it in a wastebasket labeled "Temporary Insanity." To me that is not being honest. It is not true. It is not justice.

I maintain that it is wrong for the criminal attorneys and judges to stand in our courts and allow murderers to go free on the basis of temporary insanity.

In Florida, there was one case in which a college professor was shot and killed by a student. Two court-appointed psychiatrists concluded the killer to have been insane at the time of the shooting; then later they declared him competent to stand trial. According to these psychiatrists, the man was insane one day but sane a few weeks later.

How honest can such findings be? The human mind cannot be twisted around like that. It cannot be a certain way one moment and a different way another moment.

One of the cases we referred to in chapter 2 involved "the Yorkshire Ripper." In this case thirteen women were brutally murdered in the Yorkshire area of England over a period of five years.

Is Peter Sutcliffe, the man responsible for these horrible killings, a lunatic? Is he crazy? Insane?

For these five years he continued to carry on his business. He made a living. How can he be a lunatic?

Apparently, "the Yorkshire Ripper" conducted himself as a normal person, doing normal things, until a strange compulsion came upon him. Then he had to go out and find a woman to kill.

Can such a person be "temporarily insane"?

I say, No.

I have been inside prisons and talked with people who have committed murder. Some say they just didn't know

45

what they were doing at that moment. But they did know. They were fulfilling that desire to kill inside them and they knew what they were doing.

Let's not permit ourselves to be deceived. There is too much unprovoked murder in the world today for us to let it go any longer. If there were only one or two people killed each year, it might be different. But these stories are in our newspapers and on our TV news broadcasts every day. Then when it happens next door, we have no choice: we must face the stark reality.

It happened in our neighborhood. Our paper boy slipped out of bed one night, went next door, and murdered the lady who lived there – a widow who had done nice things for him. He stabbed her to death, went home, and crawled back into bed, still wearing his bloody clothes.

You can say that he was "crazy," but his school-teachers would disagree. He wasn't crazy; he could learn. There was something else.

What was it?

5
Is Capital Punishment Murder?

When a person is found guilty of unprovoked murder, what happens then?

Today we live in a doubleminded society. If someone kills one of our loved ones, we angrily demand the death sentence. But when somebody else is killed, we say, "Well, maybe we shouldn't send him to the electric chair. After all, capital punishment is inhuman."

There is a segment of American society today which vocally opposes the use of the death sentence by force of governmental decree.

In 1967, the Unites States Supreme Court announced it would take capital punishment under advisement. At that point the lower courts in the nation were obligated to place the question of capital punishment in limbo. They were unable to enforce it until they received orders from the highest court.

In 1972, five years later, the Supreme Court voted that the death penalty laws in forty-one of the fifty states were unconstitutional on the grounds that they were applied arbitrarily and in a discriminatory manner.

In the decade from 1967 to 1977, the number of violent murders more than doubled on a per capita basis.

The opponents of the death penalty claim that death by governmental decree is cruel and unusual punishment, and thus is prohibited by the Constitution of the United States.

God's Answer Is Definite

Revelation 13:10 says, *He that killeth with the sword must be killed with the sword.* You may disagree with this statement or with other statements in the Bible, but that doesn't change a thing.

You can disagree with the law of gravity; but if you jump off a ten-story building, you will find the law of gravity still very much in effect. The only thing changed is your body when it hits the ground!

All of us must realize that the laws of God were set into motion before we were born, and they will continue in motion after we are gone. We have nothing to do with them, except to either obey or disobey them.

What God Has To Say

According to the Bible, it was God who first inaugurated capital punishment. In the first book of the Bible, the Book of Genesis, God said:

And surely your blood of your lives will I require; at the hand of every beast will I require it, and at the hand of man; at the hand of every man's brother will I require the life of man.

Whoso sheddeth man's blood, by man shall his blood be shed: for in the image of God made he man.

Genesis 9:5,6

According to this, a willful murder had to be judged. God said so. One life had to be given for another. Even when a beast killed a human, the beast had to die.

These words were not given just for those days. In verse 12 of the same chapter, God sealed the matter by saying:

This is the token of the covenant which I make between me and you and every living creature that is with you, for perpetual generations.

Is Capital Punishment Murder?

God was very careful in the Scriptures to pronounce capital punishment in the exact manner that it was to be applied.

In the second book of the Bible, the Book of Exodus, it says, *He that smiteth a man, so that he die, shall be surely put to death* (Exodus 21:12).

In the Book of Leviticus, chapter 24, verses 17-22, we read:

And he that killeth any man shall surely be put to death.

And he that killeth a beast shall make it good; beast for beast.

And if a man cause a blemish in his neighbour; as he hath done, so shall it be done to him;

Breach for breach, eye for eye, tooth for tooth: as he hath caused a blemish in a man, so shall it be done to him again.

And he that killeth a beast, he shall restore it: and he that killeth a man, he shall be put to death.

Ye shall have one manner of law, as well for the stranger, as for one of your own country: for I am the Lord your God.

This was a divine law relating to both man and beast. It applied to every hurt that could be suffered.

In the Book of Numbers, chapter 35, verses 9-15, we read:

And the Lord spake unto Moses, saying,

Speak unto the children of Israel, and say unto them, When ye be come over Jordan into the land of Canaan;

Then ye shall appoint you cities to be cities of refuge for you; that the slayer may flee thither, which killeth any person at unawares.

And they shall be unto you cities for refuge from the avenger; that the manslayer die not, until he stand before the congregation in judgment.

And of these cities which ye shall give six cities shall ye have for refuge.

Ye shall give three cities on this side Jordan, and three cities shall ye give in the land of Canaan, which shall be cities of refuge.

These six cities shall be a refuge, both for the children of Israel, and for the stranger, and for the sojourner among them: that every one that killeth any person unawares may flee thither.

God appointed six cities as places of refuge. If anyone killed another person in error or unwillingly, he could flee to one of these cities and find peace and protection. He would be safe there until he could stand before the judges.

Exodus 21:22 says, *If men strive, and hurt a woman with child, so that her fruit depart from her, and yet no mischief follow: he shall be surely punished, according as the woman's husband will lay upon him; and he shall pay as the judges determine.*

In other words, if neither the pregnant woman nor the unborn child are harmed, the woman's husband will determine punishment.

Verse 23 says, *If any mischief follow, then thou shalt give life for life.* If either the baby or the mother dies, then there is an automatic penalty: a life for a life.

No doubt some people will dispute this on the grounds that it is taken from the Old Testament. In Acts 25:10,11, the Apostle Paul said:

I stand at Caesar's judgment seat, where I ought to be judged: to the Jews have I done no wrong, as thou very well knowest.

For if I be an offender, or have committed any thing worthy of death, I refuse not to die: but if there be none of these things whereof these accuse me, no man may deliver me unto them. I appeal unto Caesar.

To Cleanse the Land

The Bible clearly teaches that when a person willingly takes another person's life, he automatically forfeits his own life. God knew this was the only means by which He could uphold the sacredness of human life.

Both Old and New Testaments instruct that the payment of a murderer's life must be taken to fulfill this obligation. But such payment is to be taken by the civil authorities, not by individuals.

The civil government is responsible before God. When it does not fulfill its obligation, it becomes weakened and begins to die.

Capital punishment was established by God to protect the innocent and to maintain a correct society. When it is not enforced, all individuals in that society become threatened.

God was very careful to point out that murder pollutes the land. Numbers 35:33,34 says:

> *So ye shall not pollute the land wherein ye are: for blood it defileth the land: and the land cannot be cleansed of the blood that is shed therein, but by the blood of him that shed it.*
>
> *Defile not therefore the land which ye shall inhabit, wherein I dwell: for I the Lord dwell among the children of Israel.*

In God's eyes, the only way to cleanse that land is with the death penalty.

Capital punishment *must* be enforced, but never abused. It must never be enforced in a spirit of anger or hate, but always in obedience to the Word of God, with one goal in mind: to keep the land clean from evil.

Love and the Death Penalty

There has developed in Christianity a completely false attitude toward the death penalty.

Many people contend that because God tells us not to kill and not to hate, the death penalty is not of God. They say that the government has no right to perform the laws of God. But people who feel this way have missed the point.

In the New Testament there are many passages that teach the Christian to love and forgive. Jesus specifically said that if a man hurts you, you are to turn the other cheek.

These rules are good and true, but they apply only on a personal basis between individuals. God has set up governments to carry out the laws of the land.

The Bible teaches that we are not to personally show hatred to others, but it also says that we are not to permit criminals to destroy our people indiscriminately.

In the Bible, the death angel went through Egypt one night, and the firstborn in every family died. God did that as a penalty against Egypt for the enslavement of an entire nation. The Israelites had been held in bondage and their children had died at the hands of the Egyptians.

In the Old Testament, King Saul lost his kingdom because he did not carry out capital punishment. (1 Samuel 15.) God told Saul to take the city of Amalek and spare no one, but Saul disobeyed. He saved King Agag. So God repented for setting Saul as king over Israel and rejected him from being king.

A Price To Pay

In Numbers 35:30,31 God specifically said:
Whoso killeth any person, the murderer shall be put to death by the mouth of witnesses: but one witness

*shall not testify against any person to cause him to die.
Moreover ye shall take no satisfaction for the life of
a murderer, which is guilty of death: but he shall be
surely put to death.*

There is a price to pay when one person takes the life
of another person.

Every person should be aware *before* he commits an
act of crime that he will be required to accept and endure
the penalty for that crime. Every person must be taught
from babyhood to adulthood that when he hurts, he is to
be hurt.

It should be a clear and simple fact in every person's
thinking: You just don't take human life! You don't do it!
If you do, then you forfeit the right to live.

When you treat others wrong, you must be treated
wrong. The Bible says, *Be sure your sin will find you out*
(Numbers 32:23); and, *The wages of sin is death* (Romans
6:23). Sin receives wages, and those wages are death. The
ultimate penalty for sin is death.

We need to fit these truths into our legal system.
Today, in this country there are unregenerate persons who
are beyond rehabilitation and, therefore, have become a
burden and a danger to society.

When a person is tried for murder and a jury of his
peers is convinced of his guilt beyond a reasonable doubt,
then our government and the laws of God say that
person is worthy of capital punishment. There should be
no question about it at that point.

6
Is There Hope for the Criminally Possessed?

Is there hope for a person once he has committed murder? Is there hope for the criminally possessed people in the world?

Yes!

Being a person of positive life and action, and having faith in God, I know there is hope for any and every human being living on the face of this earth.

The Thief Was Saved

Many people saw Jesus Christ die on the cross. Many heard His words. But only one man found eternal life that day. The only person converted at the cross of Jesus was a criminal: a thief who was hanging on one of the crosses next to Jesus. That person turned to Jesus and said, *Lord, remember me when thou comest into thy kingdom* (Luke 23:42).

When Jesus heard those words coming from the heart of a thief, He did not scold him because of the crimes he had committed. He simply turned to him and said, *To day shalt thou be with me in paradise* (Luke 23:43).

God will save anyone who will turn to Him – no matter how deep into sin they may have gone. Any person who is truly sorry and turns to God in repentance can be saved.

I am a very positive person. I live a positive life. I have positive actions and faith in a positive God. I believe that God can save any human being upon the face of this earth – whoever he might be.

God *can* save. He *wants* to save. He *will* save.

"Chiefest of Sinners" Saved

God's desire to reach out and pull man up from his sin is evident in the life of the Apostle Paul.

Before he was saved, Paul (then known as Saul of Tarsus) was responsible for putting both men and women in jail. (Acts 8:3.) He stood by and affirmed the death of Stephen. (Acts 7:58-8:1.) He may have even murdered many people, having been involved in the great outburst of hostility against the infant Christian Church in Jerusalem.

But while on his way to Damascus to destroy the Church there, Saul had a vision of Christ:

There shined round about him a light from heaven: and he fell to the earth, and heard a voice saying unto him, Saul, Saul, why persecutest thou me?

Acts 9:3,4

At that moment Saul surrendered to the Lord and became an apostle of the Lord Jesus Christ. Then the man who called himself the chiefest of sinners was converted and wrote most of the New Testament.

That is what God did for Paul, who in his own words was a murderer, a persecutor, and a blasphemer. (1 Timothy 1:13; Galatians 1:13.)

If God can do that, He can save any criminal in any penitentiary. Just because a person has done wrong does not mean that he cannot become good. God wants to save everyone, even the criminally possessed.

There are people who say, "I've done too much that is wrong. I can't be forgiven." That is not true. No human being can sin too far, not if he still has life and sincerely wants God.

Those who sin against the Holy Ghost don't want God,

or the Bible, or the Church, or good people. They are against everything pure and holy.

Murder is not a sin that is beyond salvation. Many murderers have been saved, but they had to turn their hearts to God. There is no person beyond His redemptive hand, but they must reach up and place their hand in His.

There *is* hope for the criminally possessed – those who have brought destruction, those who have hurt others, those who have committed murder.

There is hope in the Lord Jesus Christ. He saved the Apostle Paul and transformed him into a precious minister of the Word – and He will do the same for people today.

He will deliver a possessed spirit from the clutches of demonic power.

He will renew a warped mind through the power of His Word.

Why?

Because He cares for all men. But they must permit Him to come into their lives. He will not force His way in. Even Saul of Tarsus had to willingly open his heart and receive the Lord Jesus into his life that day on the road to Damascus.

Our ministry reaches into more than one hundred prisons in the United States. Chaplains have shared how our teachings have been received by prisoners on death row, men who are awaiting execution.

They receive our teachings because we tell it like it is. We are bold to tell them how Jesus Christ loves and cares for them, how He is reaching out to them.

They have transgressed. They have stepped across the line. They have taken another person's life, and the government may be required to carry out the death penalty that was imposed on them.

But God will save those who put their trust in Him,

regardless of what they may have done. If they will turn to God in true repentance, He will meet them there and cleanse their souls of sin.

Sin Cannot Be Hidden

If you try to hide your sins, God will reveal them. *Be sure your sin will find you out* (Numbers 32:23).

I remember an incident that occurred when I was a boy that serves as an excellent example of this Scripture truth. A man killed his neighbor, wrapped a chain around him, and dropped his body into one of the log ponds at the saw mill. The man who died was named Mr. Rice.

There was no explanation for Mr. Rice's disappearance. Because his body was not found, his wife thought he had run off and left her; so after a period of years she was remarried.

Ten years went by.

Then one day the murderer, who as working at the log pond, said to a fellow worker, "I buried a grain of rice in these waters ten years ago, and it didn't sprout."

The man he was talking to began to think of how his friend, Mr. Rice, had disappeared ten years ago and had never been found. He went to the legal authorities with his story, and a new investigation was begun. They decided to drag the pond; and when they did, a man's skeleton was found with a chain wrapped around it.

After all those years, the man who killed Mr. Rice was put in prison. His sin ultimately found him out. I don't know what happened to him, whether he received the death sentence or a prolonged prison term; but he paid a penalty for his actions.

The devil won't let you keep quiet. That man had to make some remark, even if only in jest. If you try to hide your deeds, you will never make it. Your sins will find you out.

The Bible says some men's judgment goes ahead and some men's judgment follows after. (1 Timothy 5:24.) If you don't confess and ask forgiveness, you will have to stand before God and answer for it. So many unsolved murders will be accounted for at the great judgment seat of God. Many hidden mysteries will come to light at that time.

My friend, if there is anything in your life that is hidden, I want you at this moment to ask God to forgive you for it. Ask God to come into your heart and into your life.

7

Can a Human Be Possessed
by a Satanic Entity?

To properly answer the question of whether a human being can be possessed by a satanic entity, we first have to understand how a human is designed.

Man's Threefold Existence

There are three parts in man's being: spirit, soul, and body. The soul is where I want us to focus our attention.

Within the realm of the soul, there are three parts: the mind, the will, and the emotions. These three great deciding factors – mind, will, and emotions – come to us through the Adamic nature we possess, and they will be either the cardinal strengths or weaknesses of our total being.

The mind functions remarkably as the primary guide to our lives.

The emotions include the vast areas of feeling: temper, anger, happiness, contentment, etc. If not stabilized, man's emotions will run out of control.

The will governs man's decision-making process and controls how he acts, whether good or bad.

If these three elements of the human soul are not given over to God, they will be taken under the control of the devil.

Strength of the Human Mind

Within the realm of the soul, the most powerful element is the mind. The human mind is the citadel and stronghold of a person's soul, leading, guiding, and directing his life.

The mind is capable of moving in any direction to learn and to train itself. Through the mind, a person can become a farmer by learning about soil and seed. He can learn medicine and become a doctor, or learn law and become an attorney.

There is no limit to the knowledge that can be accumulated through the facets of the human mind. We see this today in a world that is exploding with remarkable and amazing discoveries.

Without doubt, the mind is the most outstanding factor in the human personality.

The Mind Must Choose

The Lord Jesus Christ said specifically that man should serve God with his mind. (Luke 10:27.) If we don't serve God with our minds, then we will serve another entity – a personality unlike God, a personality that is not good or kind or holy or righteous.

Every human mind on the face of the earth serves some entity whether it be good or evil, whether it be God or the devil. Each person must make his own decision as to which of the two he will choose to serve.

With your rational mind, you can make the decision to serve the Almighty God.

You can think about God: calculating His greatness and His majesty, recognizing Him and honoring Him as Creator of the stars and the seas and the mountains.

You can understand God and know that He is the heavenly Father, that He is *your* Father. You can love Him and draw nigh to Him, knowing that He is never far from you and that He cares for you.

You can let every day be a day when you give service to God – praising Him, worshiping Him, blessing His creation.

You can choose to serve such a God, or you can choose to serve another god – the god of this world, the god who controls the negative things of this world – but that will only lead to a satanic situation in your life.

Just as the human mind can be directed in its positive relationships, it can also be directed in its negative relationships. A person can be possessed with either good or evil.

I am a possessed person: possessed of God. I know exactly when I became possessed. I was a sinner, away from God and loving the devil; but I made the decision to give myself over to the entity called God. When I divested myself of the influences of the devil, refusing to serve him any longer, I became a new person through the power of God that had entered my life.

You must decide the same in your own life.

Too many Americans have said, "I will live bad. I want to live bad. I desire to live bad." In so doing, they hurt themselves, their community, and society as a whole; but, most of all, they affect their own eternity.

God wants you to serve Him, to love Him. You can serve God with that positive relationship and be possessed of His goodness and love; or you can serve the devil with a negative relationship and be possessed with an entity of evil that is far beyond human strength.

You must choose!

In truly understanding this, there are three facts that must be realized.

The Devil Is Real

A person must come to know that there is an entity of evil commonly known as "the devil."

As long as a person or a society denies this fact, it will be impossible for them to understand what really happens to many thousands of human beings – not just those found to be criminals, but others who are intensely jealous or go crazy with anger.

For instance, a wife may become so consumed with jealousy that she throws dishes against the wall, and some men get so angry that they kick doors or break furniture.

These people are under the influence of "something." But what?

Their actions are not normal or natural for a human being. They certainly are not under the influence of a loving heavenly Father. So there must be something else, another power or force to consider.

If such actions are not the result of God's power or human power, there is only one power left: satanic power. The devil is real!

The Devil Is Evil

Once we recognize that there is an entity called Satan or the devil, then it is necessary to identify him.

Very simply, Satan is the source of all evil, of all that is bad and ungodly. The devil hates God. He is angry at God.

There is a war going on between the forces of good and evil, a battle that is cosmic and demonic. It began when an archangel named Lucifer (or Satan) was dethroned. It will continue until Jesus Christ returns to earth, redeems the earth from Satan's power, and throws Satan into the lake of fire for eternity.

Until then, the devil will strike out at God the best

way he knows how, and that is by trying to hurt the object of God's love: you and me.

I have three sons and eleven grandchildren. The best way to hurt me would not be by striking out at me directly, but by hurting those closest to me.

To the devil a human being means absolutely nothing. Satan has no interest in humans, either positively or negatively. Mass murder is one method he has devised to destroy that which God has made. He stands back, laughing, and says to God, "See. That's Your image. But look at what I've done to him."

Crime and sin are ways the devil has of mocking God. All he wants to do is get at God through us. By dominating us, he takes God's place in our lives.

It is remarkable to me how people in Africa and Asia can worship the devil as they do. They worship an entity that shows absolutely no regard for them. He won't provide for them. He won't give them a good harvest. He won't do anything except push them down into the muck and mire of their human existence, taking them as deeply into nothingness as he can.

The devil has no regard for those who serve him. Only God loves the people who serve Him and look to Him as their provider. Until people realize this, they will continue to wander in a labyrinth of confusion in the world.

The Devil Can Possess a Human

The devil is real, he is evil, and he has the potential power to possess a person's mental faculties and emotions.

In the Roland Kashney case (see chapter 2) in which two people were murdered in Chicago, the defense was based on Kashney's contention that he was under the influence of demonic forces when he confessed to having committed those murders.

Both prosecution and defense attorneys in this case requested that I give what they called "expert witness" regarding the subject of demon possession. I was subpoenaed to appear in the Cook County Criminal Court and testify of my experiences with demonic forces.

These legal minds were endeavoring to discover if it is possible for a human being to come under the strange influence and power of an entity outside the realm of human existence.

Without hesitation, my answer was a most definite *YES.*

8
Demon-Possessed People
I have Known

My first observance of demon power came when I was in my early twenties. I had joined evangelist Howard Carter of London and, together, we were traveling through many countries, teaching and preaching the gospel of Jesus.

During these travels, we spent three months in Java, Indonesia. While there I was engaged to speak at a local church and during the song service that evening, I saw a demonic manifestation.

A young girl about twelve or thirteen years of age left her chair and began to writhe on the floor like a serpent. She would stick out her tongue as her face was drawn in all kinds of terrible expressions. A repulsive green foam began to ooze from her mouth.

The Javanese minister in charge of the service paid no attention to her and continued with the service.

When I walked to the pulpit, God told me to speak freedom to that girl. Although I had never experienced such a thing, I said firmly, "Get back on that seat."

Though the Indonesian girl did not understand English, the devil within her did. Instantly, she returned to her seat and sat motionless while I preached the message. At the close of my sermon, I prayed for her deliverance in the name of Jesus. That transfixed look left her eyes. She relaxed and smiled. There was no struggle.

All my words to her were in English. I did not use the interpreter, but the devil understood. He knew I had authority over him through the Lord Jesus Christ.

The Invisible Boy

One of the strangest situations I have encountered through many years of worldwide ministry involved a young Philippine boy named Cornelio who was about twelve years of age.

It seems that Cornelio had an unusual habit of disappearing into thin air. He could be sitting in the dining room with his family and simply disappear. Not a door or window would move. At other times, he would be playing with his brothers and sisters in the front room. Suddenly they would cry, "Cornelio is gone!"

At school one day, Cornelio disappeared while writing on the blackboard. I have testimony from his schoolteacher about it. It so alarmed and frightened her that she suffered a nervous breakdown and never sufficiently recovered to teach school again.

These strange disappearances caused his family much consternation. They were members of the Roman Catholic Church and had no idea what to do about these occurrences.

Together with their minister, Cornelio's parents brought the boy to one of my meetings in Manila. When they described the situation to me, I immediately realized the satanic power involved. When I looked directly into Cornelio's eyes, I could see that he was demon possessed.

I laid my hands on him and prayed for God to break the power that this evil spirit had in Cornelio's life. Then I prayed for his salvation. After praying for his deliverance, I was exhausted physically; but I was sure that God had answered my prayer. From that moment forward, the boy never disappeared again.

A short time later I was able to spend some time with Cornelio and his family. He told me then in detail about his strange disappearances.

Approximately a year before, Cornelio had been walking across a field on his way home from school when he saw a girl in a white dress. She was very pretty with beautiful long hair. She came up to him, smiled, and said, "Please go for a walk with me."

He said they spent much time together. Whenever she touched him, both of them would become invisible. They walked for hours, sometimes all night and all day, never getting tired. Then when she touched him again, he would become visible.

While questioning Cornelio, I asked if he had ever felt the body of the girl. He said, "Yes, she was always cold, never warm."

When I asked about the manner in which she enticed him to go with her, he seemed a little frightened. He said she was very demanding, that she would grab him and become angry if he did not obey her every wish.

I asked if anyone else had seen this girl. He told how he was the only person who could see her and that she was standing near him most of the time.

At this point I began to question Cornelio more intently. In answer to my probings, he admitted that the "girl" was not really a girl at all and that "she" was not even young.

He said there were many times that she asked him to go away with her and never return. But he would not go.

He seemed happy to be delivered from that "presence" and said, "I used to see her all the time. The night you prayed for me she was standing at the church door, begging me to come with her. But I have not seen her since that night. I am glad God has set me free."

Today Cornelio is leading a normal life.

The Brazilian Witch Doctor

In my travels throughout the world, I have met human beings who were not senile or feebleminded, stupid or insane. Yet their actions at times were inhuman. They were possessed with an entity beyond themselves.

One such person was a Brazilian witch doctor. His business was witchcraft. Before he was born, he had been baptized to the devil by a witch doctor and dedicated to certain spirits. Warm chicken blood from a slaughtered chicken was placed upon the naked belly of his mother a few weeks before he was born.

Soon after his birth, it was very apparent that these spirits controlled him.

At age two under the power of the devil, he could write out prescriptions in Latin for people seeking medical help to take to the local druggist. He could not read his native language of Portuguese, nor did he bother to look at what he had written – he couldn't read it! But the druggist who filled Latin prescriptions read and filled the prescriptions he wrote.

As a witch doctor, he brought not only curses upon people, but healings as well. He committed many crimes, doing all kinds of horrible and demonic things under the power of witchcraft. At night he would slit the throat of a chicken and drink its blood.

Though this man was very active as a witch doctor, he was also very civilized and held a position in the office of the President of Brazil. Each day, dressed in a tuxedo and white gloves, he would greet guests and usher them into the President's office.

What a contrast! A respectable government employee during the day; a professional witch doctor at night.

No doubt psychologists and legal experts would say the man lived a "Jekyll and Hyde" existence, that he possessed a split personality.

But when this witch doctor was prayed for by a minister of the gospel, he was instantly set free from the power of all evil entities. He became a new person.

When I brought him to America, he traveled from Florida to the state of Washington, testifying of his conversion. He has now given up his work in the executive office of his country and is a minister of the gospel.

Clarita Villanueva

One case of demon possession that was given great news coverage at the time occurred at Bilibid Prison in the Philippine Islands.

A seventeen-year-old harlot named Clarita Villanueva had been picked up off the streets of Manila at 2:00 a.m. for soliciting trade and was placed in Bilibid Prison.

Bitten by Demons

Within forty-eight hours, unusual things began to happen. On many areas of her flesh there appeared humanlike teeth marks, deep impressions with blood running from them. There were marks on the back of her neck, the back of her arm, her shoulder and hips – places that were impossible for her to reach.

The six doctors on staff at the prison called in a number of physicians and psychiatrists. They found Clarita to be completely sane at her rational times; but when this entity, which came to be known as "The Thing," would bite her or possess her, supernatural phenomenon would occur.

The man in charge of medicine at the prison, Dr. Mariano Lara, was highly educated and experienced in the medical field. He was professor and head of pathology and legal medicine at Manila Central University as well as professional lecturer of legal medicine at the University of Santo Tomas.

Through thirty-eight years of practicing medicine, Dr. Lara had never accepted the existence of any nonmaterial force in the universe. At first, he paid no special attention to the reports of his two assistants about the strange occurrences surrounding their new prisoner. He concluded that the attacks were epileptic and thought the girl should be transferred to the psychiatric hospital.

However, when Dr. Lara was present during one session with Clarita Villanueva, he was able to see for himself the humanlike bite impressions on her body. He later recounted the incident to me, describing it as a frightening experience.

When first brought into the office, Clarita was unconscious, in a trancelike state. As Dr. Lara closely examined her body and scrutinized the bite marks on her skin, she began to recover from the trance.

Unable to stand up by herself, one of Dr. Lara's medical assistants, Alfonso Aquino, took hold of her and placed her on a bed. When he put his hands on her arms, she began to scream as if in dreadful pain.

In relating the incident to me, Dr. Lara said, "When I removed Alfonso's hand from Clarita, I saw with unbelief a great number of teethlike marks as from the upper and lower jaws of a human. It was moist in the area bitten. Even with my unbelieving eyes, I could not understand or explain how they were produced."

Clarita continued to scream for about fifteen minutes. Then she began to turn blue in the face as if being choked, and reddish welts appeared on the front of her neck. Again, she went into a trance that lasted about ten minutes.

When she regained consciousness and became normal again, she was able to talk with a group of interns, answering their questions sanely and intelligently.

When Dr. Lara asked her who was causing the bites

on her body, she told of two "beings" that were alternately biting her. She described one as a big, black hairy, human-like fellow, very tall, with two sharp canine teeth and a long beard like a Hindu. She said his feet were three times the size of normal human feet. The other creature was very small, about two or three feet tall, and also black, hairy, and ugly.

Faith vs. Science

At the time of this incident I was living with my family in Manila while founding a church there. Having heard of this strange occurrence over the radio, I was deeply disturbed as my heart cried out for this girl.

Doctors and psychiatrists were trying to cure her through medical means; but I knew she was demon possessed, and the only cure was for her to be delivered through the power of God and the name of Jesus.

While in prayer for the girl, I sensed the Lord leading me to go pray for her. After praying all night, God spoke to my heart and said, "If you will go to the jail and pray for her, I will deliver her."

My immediate response was, "No."

However, I found that I could no longer pray for her with a clear conscience. I was not being sincere before the Lord. If I truly wanted her to be delivered, I had to be willing to go there myself and pray for her. Finally, I decided to go to Bilibid Prison.

Through a network of political connections, I was able to gain entrance into the prison and speak with Dr. Lara. He was the person who would have to grant permission for me to pray for Clarita.

My first objective was to convince Dr. Lara that I was capable of helping Clarita. Since he possessed such a scientific mind and rejected the idea of spiritual phe-nomena, I decided to begin my argument there.

In speaking with him, I explained the existence of three powers in the universe: positive (which is God), human (which is man), and negative (which is the devil).

Dr. Lara admitted that Clarita's behavior could not be attributed to a positive power nor could it be considered human; but because of his many years of medical experience, he could not simply accept the explanation as being "supernatural."

I continued by pointing out how a negative force could not have control over a positive force; that if evil was mightier than good, our universe would no longer exist.

Then I read Jesus' words from the Gospel of Mark, chapter 16, verse 17: *And these signs shall follow them that believe; In my name shall they cast out devils.*

I was bold in my presentation of Christian authority, explaining how Clarita without doubt was under the influence of demonic power and that the Lord Jesus Christ was able to deliver her from it.

Dr. Lara agreed to let me pray for her, and an appointment was made for me to meet with her the next morning.

Clarita Pronounces Death

Before I became involved in the case of Clarita Villanueva, there were some truly frightening manifestations of demonic power through her.

The newspapers had picked up the story and sent reporters to investigate. One of them that came to Bilibid Prison to interview Clarita was Manuel Ramos. Ramos was very outspoken in his unbelief of the matter and made sport of the idea, stating that he believed it to be a hoax.

While Ramos was making fun of her, Clarita mumbled, "You will die."

The next day at the very same hour, Manuel Ramos was pronounced dead of a heart attack.

Captain Anthony Ganibi, the chief officer of Bilibid Prison, was Clarita's official custodian. There were many encounters between them during the three weeks of these manifestations.

One day Clarita said, "Captain, don't worry me any more or it will be your neck."

Captain Ganibi suddenly began to lose weight. Though the doctors did their best to assist him, he became like a wilted flower and eventually died.

I happened to be at Bilibid Prison when his funeral procession left for the cemetery. Dr. Lara said, "This is a strange story of the death of our Captain."

Deliverance in Jesus' Name

If she were in our country today, I expect Clarita Villanueva would have been put under the influence of drugs and placed in a padded cell. The news media would never have known about it.

In fact, today in America, there may be thousands like her in our padded cells: human beings, absolutely naked and living like animals, eating their food with their hands – food that is pushed to them underneath bars.

We say they are demented and crazy, but they are not. The devil has entered into them to destroy them. That is what happened to Clarita Villanueva.

The day I went to Bilibid Prison to pray for Clarita, there was a group of perhaps a hundred spectators – newsmen, police officers, photographers, even some prisoners. Much curiosity had been raised about this man who had come to pray for a girl he called "demon possessed."

When we had gathered together in the chapel, Dr. Lara had Clarita brought in. When she entered the room, she looked closely at each person. When she came to me at the end of the line, her expression changed. She glared at me and said, "I don't like you!"

75

I had her to sit on a wooden bench, and I pulled up a chair in front of her.

There followed a confrontation between the powers of God and the devil. The demons spoke through her lips and used the vilest language to curse me, God, the Holy Spirit, and the blood of Jesus.

The words coming from Clarita's lips were in English; but later I had to use an interpreter for she could not speak English.

That morning I experienced the greatest battle of my life. We spent hours in a verbal confrontation.

The demons would scream and curse God. I would rebuke them in the name of Jesus, demanding that they leave her body and telling them how God is holy.

They would curse the blood of Jesus. I would rebuke them, reminding them of how Jesus had authority over every evil power and how His blood is holy.

When they would curse the Holy Spirit, I would rebuke them and tell them how God's Spirit is holy.

When they would curse me, I would rebuke them, telling them how the power of God was within me.

Eventually, it seemed that deliverance had come. The demons quit talking to me and the biting stopped. But I knew that the battle was not over.

It was nearly noon. I was soaked with perspiration and nearly exhausted. I told Dr. Lara I would go home, spend the next day fasting and praying, and return the day after.

When I arrived at Bilibid, I was told that Clarita had not been bitten since I had prayed for her. But I knew she had not been delivered.

When the devils saw me, they immediately began to cry, "Go away! Go away!"

I answered them in the authority of the Lord Jesus

Christ, "No, I will not go away. You are going away! This girl will be delivered today!"

Again there followed a battle, but it was different this time. The devils knew they would have to go.

When they finally departed, Clarita relaxed. The demonic glare left her eyes and she smiled. It was an emotional time. Some of the reporters and doctors were weeping, giving evidence of how terrific the battle had been.

When I asked Clarita if the demons were gone, she answered in her own language, "Yes."

"Where did they go?"

She replied, "Out that window."

The Demons Return

As we were preparing to leave, Clarita screamed and the glare returned to her eyes. I knew the devils had come back.

I said to them, "Why have you returned? You know you must go and not return."

Through her lips came these words in English, "But she is unclean. We have a right to live in her."

In a strong voice, I answered, "Mary Magdalene was unclean with seven like you, but Jesus came into her life. She became clean by His mighty power. So I command you to depart now and Jesus will make her clean."

The demons left and Clarita became normal again. I explained to her what had happened and had her pray with me for the forgiveness of her sins.

A short time later, the same thing happened again. The demons returned saying, "She has not asked us to go. She wants us. It is only you who desire for us to leave."

Again, I demanded them to leave, and they left immediately. Then I had Clarita to demand that they leave and never return. When she did, I taught her to pray and plead the blood of Jesus against them.

Before I left Clarita, I warned her that the demons would try to return, but that she must demand that they leave.

They did return to attack her; and when she commanded them to leave, a strange thing happened. After struggling against them, Clarita went into a coma with her fists clenched. As Dr. Lara pried open her hands, he found some long, black hair of a coarse texture.

Under the microscope Dr. Lara discovered that this hair was not from the body of a human. Here was a mystery the doctor could not explain. How could an invisible being lose a hair that becomes visible when it is pulled out by a human being?

Clarita Is Free

When Clarita came before the judge to be tried on charges of vagrancy and prostitution, she told of her deliverance. The judge placed her in a home for wayward girls for observation.

While she was there, Dr. Lara and I visited her twice. Both times she was excited and happy to see us. As we talked with her, it was obvious that she was not the same girl who had been kept at Bilibid Prison. The girl at Bilibid was tormented and tortured by demonic power. This girl was perfectly normal. There was no doubt that she had been delivered from satanic power and had recovered from the nightmare of demon possession.

When Clarita was paroled, she stayed in the home of a Christian family for a time, then moved to a small town away from Manila and settled there.

The story of Clarita Villanueva's deliverance is outstanding. Through this miracle, great revival came to the nation of the Philippines and the city of Manila.

9
Cultism and Unprovoked Murder

The Apostle Paul, under inspiration of the Holy Spirit, wrote some very remarkable words in his first epistle to Timothy: *The Spirit speaketh expressly, that in the latter times some shall depart from the faith, giving heed to seducing spirits, and doctrines of devils* (1 Timothy 4:1).

These words were written by the power of the Holy Ghost, and you and I should listen very carefully to them.

There are situations in the world today that are exactly what this scripture is speaking of. People have departed from the faith. They no longer have faith in God. They have taken on something else in its place – a strangeness and a peculiarity that is not human.

Cultism and spiritism have become very popular among certain segments of our society. These people go about their daily work in a normal fashion, but religiously they are under a negative influence that is superhuman.

Do cultism and spiritism have any direct relationship to unprovoked murder?

If you study the purposes and the reasons for unprovoked murder, especially those involving multiple murders, you will discover that in so many of the cases cultism is a basic element. The people responsible are involved in the occult and, therefore, are under the influence of demonic spirits.

The Manson case in California is an example. (See chapter 2.) The Manson "family" was so deeply involved in demon worship that they were performing blood sacrifices. Charles Manson's followers were actually deifying him and, in doing so, they delivered themselves over to the influence of demonic powers.

We can see this also in the case of John Wayne Gacy of Chicago, who was found guilty of murdering thirty-three young men and boys. (See chapter 2.) According to Gacy, there were four personalities, or spirits, within him who made him kill these young people. He was dealing in the spirit world with demons, and the result was the largest group of murders in American history.

In most cases, Gacy could not identify his victims. He didn't know them and had no animosities toward them. The conflict was totally within himself. John Gacy ended up being strapped down in a mental hospital to live with his memories.

Perhaps the most hideous waste of human life as a result of cultism occurred with Jim Jones and the mass suicide in Guyana, South America. (See chapter 2.) With demonic control comes total deception, and the Jones' massacre is an excellent example.

What began many years ago as a sincere effort for good in a young minister gradually became warped and perverted. As Jones' own ideas and thoughts became uppermost to him, the devil was able to make inroads in his life. The final result was a satanic deception that led 900 people to their deaths. Sheer waste!

The Church's Responsibility

It is clear that the responsibility for the problems of our times is not related solely to the courts and the judicial system, but part must be laid at the doorstep of the Church.

In the Gospel of Mark, chapter 16, Jesus Christ said in the Great Commission to the Church:

> *Go ye into all the world, and preach the gospel to every creature.*
> *He that believeth and is baptized shall be saved; but he that believeth not shall be damned.*
> *And these signs shall follow them that believe; In my name shall they cast out devils. . . .*
> Verses 15-17

According to these words of the Lord Jesus, anyone with the Spirit of God within him has the capability of relieving a person of a demon spirit through exorcism. According to First John 4:4, He Who is in us is greater than he who is in the world. As Christians, we can truly set people free from the power of the devil.

We cannot pass all the responsibility on to the judges and attorneys. The Church has a responsibility here. We must not fail this generation by being so cowardly that we will not face the issues of our time or the problems of our society.

In order to truly and completely solve situations like the Manson and Gacy murder cases, we must leave the courts and delve into the realm of the spirit. We must identify these situations properly and fight them at their source, which is demon power.

When Jesus' disciples failed at casting out an evil spirit from a child, He told them it was because they had not prepared themselves. He said, *This kind goeth not out but by prayer and fasting* (Matthew 17:21).

Perhaps the Church in America has not prepared itself spiritually for conflict by strengthening itself with God's power. The Lord Jesus said that if you are to enter a strong man's house and spoil his goods, you must first bind the strong man. (Matthew 12:29.)

If the Church does not have the power to bind the forces of evil, which is the devil, then it cannot set people free.

But the Church does have the power! God's people are stronger than the forces of evil in the world.

Standing in the Face of Demons

I prayed for a man in South America who said he was Napoleon.

I asked, "Do you go out to war?"

He said, "No, I possess this person."

"Why are you calling yourself Napoleon?"

"Because I once lived in Napoleon and made him do the things that he did. Now I am living in this man, making him do the things he does."

That demonic entity was speaking to me through that man.

I said, "You spirit that caused Napoleon to do evil and caused this man to do evil, I speak to you by the blood of Jesus Christ. I bind you, and upon the force and authority of the Great Commission, I come against you. I now exorcise you. I command you to come out and let this man go free!"

Immediately, the man was set free.

From the time of their fall from heaven, Lucifer (Satan) and his angels have gone to and fro to hurt and destroy everything God made in the universe, whether on this planet or some other planet. But God has given His people, His Church, authority over these demonic forces.

There is not one place in the Bible where you are told to be afraid of evil spirits. There is no reason for you to be afraid. You can stand victoriously against demons. The devil has no authority over those who are truly born again by the Spirit of the living God.

While dealing with a certain case in the Chicago area, I visited with an attorney who had been involved with murder cases for fifteen years. I asked him if there had ever been a time in dealing with a suspect that he was afraid. In reply, he told this story:

"There was one man I was dealing with who was okay as long as I was agreeing with him about how to get him set free.

"But when I became the devil's advocate and started showing him the weaknesses of the case, immediately he changed: his eyes enlarged, his facial muscles tightened, and a growl came up from inside him. It terrified me."

There was evidently within that man a demonic spirit that had not surfaced until that time.

Another murder case where demonic spirits were extremely active was the case of David Berkowitz, also known as "the Son of Sam." (See chapter 2.) Calling himself by several names, such as "the Duke of Death" and "the Twenty-two Disciples of Hell," Berkowitz said he was told to kill by a demon spirit.

When asked why he murdered, he said he was given a sign, a spiritual sign, and he followed it.

To his investigating attorney, he said, "I had to do what I had to do."

The Devil Demands Blood

In so many cases of multiple murder, the murderers are in some way connected with the occult.

One horrible case of murder which occurred in the Philippines involved a couple who came home from a spiritist meeting under a spell. When they walked in the door of their home, they suddenly saw their two children as demons. The devil within them said the children were demons, so the parents jumped on the bed and attacked them.

For some unknown reason, they killed their son and daughter by jabbing sticks down their throats, up their nostrils, in their eyes and ears. The children screamed until they finally died.

When the police arrived, the parents were still screaming, "They're demons! They're demons!"

It is a fact that unprovoked murder has to do with demon power, not with insanity. Very often these cases involve demon worship and blood sacrifice.

The Bible told us centuries and centuries ago that the life of the flesh is in the blood. (Leviticus 17:11.) The mystery of human life is in the blood – not in the skin or in the bones. When you take the blood from a human, you take his life.

The devil takes advantage of this. He wants blood. He desires blood. He demands blood.

The very foundation of Christianity is a blood sacrifice. God gave His Son so that He might bleed for you and me. Jesus couldn't give His life without giving His blood. He gave His life to save all of humanity.

Human life is the most precious commodity on the face of this earth. When a person becomes a destroyer of human life, then he is obeying the dictates of the devil.

Whenever you play around with evil religions – with spiritism and the occult – you will be led down a path of destruction.

A member of my church, who had been delivered from the occult, lost two fingers while at a spiritist seance. He said the spirit demanded to eat the two fingers; so, immediately, they took a knife and cut them off. The person in charge of the seance ate the fingers there in front of the man.

Because of the problems in society today, many people have been drawn into the occult sciences. They view the occult as a solution, a way out of all that faces them, but it is only a deception. The occult will not lead them out. It will only take them in deeper.

The occult sciences deal only with a negative power or spirit. A person cannot receive help there. Help will only come from the positive force which is the Originator of the universe: Almighty God.

We must study what God has to say about these things, then believe what He says, and act on what He says. God is love, and love does not kill.

10
"The Devil Made Me Do It!"

Several years ago this saying was made popular by comedian Flip Wilson: "The devil made me do it!"

True or false?

It would be very easy to always blame our problems and weaknesses on others. These days it seems that more and more people are blaming their woes, problems, and shortcomings on the devil. As we have seen in previous chapters, there are even cases of murder in which the defendant is crying out, "The devil made me do it!"

By using attorneys and legal procedures, criminals are seeking to be set free from the responsibility of their crimes by shifting the blame over on the devil.

In the case of Arne Cheyenne Johnson (see chapter 2), attorney Martin Minnella based his entire defense on the claim that the devil possessed Johnson and caused him to commit murder – to stab to death his friend, Alan Bono.

"Jekyll and Hyde" Excuse

Another strange case of murder occurred in Sacramento, California. Sometime before dawn on an August morning, Paul Miskimen woke up, walked downstairs, picked up a piece of firewood, returned to his bedroom, and struck his wife in the head as she slept. He continued to brutally beat her and then strangled her with her own stocking.

According to family, friends, and neighbors, Paul Miskimen was a great family man, a hard worker, and a good citizen of the community.

Why would he murder his wife?
They had no answer.

When confronted by police, Miskimen broke down and confessed; but he could give them no explanation as to why he would kill his wife. Then later under hypnosis and "truth serum," a Jekyll-and-Hyde type of answer began to unfold. Another "personality" within Paul Miskimen emerged and apparently was responsible for the killing.

This "Mr. Hyde" was opposite in personality from Paul Miskimen. He even had a different name, calling himself Jack Kelly. While Paul was mild-mannered, Jack was arrogant and domineering.

This case of murder never reached a courtroom. The court-appointed psychiatrists who examined Miskimen concluded unanimously that he could not be held responsible for the murder. In their report, they stated that Paul and Jack were two separate and distinct personalities, and they considered it obvious that at times Jack had determined Paul's behavior.

Based on their findings, a California Superior Court judge found Miskimen "not guilty by reason of insanity" and placed him in a state mental hospital.

Can the Devil *Make* You Do it?

In my investigation and experience through many countries of the world regarding people who were possessed of devils, I continue to discover this very important fact: Demon possession does not fully take over a person's decision-making process.

I have talked with people who were possessed of devils and they told me that the devil could make them do many things, but that he could not make them go against their own willpower.

Every human being possesses a free moral agency, a free will capability which the devil *cannot*, and God *will not*, dominate.

Your will is a part of your being that you are obligated to give account for. The only deviation from this is when a person's mind is injured or destroyed by sickness and he becomes a vegetable. In such cases, that person would be unable to work and carry on daily activities. He could not be a C.P.A. in the daytime and kill people at night.

In visiting asylums where people are restrained, I found most of them to be docile. They are not noisy. They are not dangerous. They are not demon possessed. Those are people whose minds are sick. They have no power of decision and normally are harmless.

The one case that stands out above others in my experience is the case of Clarita Villanueva, a young girl in the Philippines, to whom I was able to minister deliverance from demonic influence. (More details about this case are found in chapter 8.)

After Clarita was completely delivered, I went to court for her and had her released. For a time, she lived in the home of one of our church members, a medical doctor. During her complete recovery, I was able to talk with her about her experiences.

A number of times, I asked her, "When you were possessed of that devil, did he ever tell you to do things that you refused to do?"

She said, "Yes."

"Could he overpower you and make you do them?"

She said, "No, he had to ask me."

"Then you were possessed according to your own will?"

She answered, "Oh, yes. I was just wanting to get something I had not known before."

"What did he ask you to do that you completely refused to do?"

"He asked me to go away with him and never come back, but I refused." (No doubt this was death, but she was afraid to go.)

She had the power to resist that satanic entity. She refused to go with him and he could not force her to.

When a person wants to kill, he makes up his own mind to do it. When a man can be a doctor in the daytime and a demon-empowered person at night, that man must give an account for all of his actions. He cannot blame it on an entity completely outside himself and say, "I'm not to blame. The devil made me do it."

Another situation I encountered in the Philippines was the case of Cornelio, "the invisible boy." (See chapter 8 for details.) Through a supernatural manifestation, this boy could disappear.

After I had prayed for him to be set free, Cornelio told how a spirit would touch him and make him disappear. He described this spirit as a beautiful young girl. But after he was delivered, he saw it as a hideous monster. The spirit had deceived him.

I asked, "Did this spirit ever tell you to do things that you didn't want to do?"

"Yes, a number of times."

"Did you refuse?"

"Yes. She told me to go away with her and never come back. I was afraid, so I wouldn't go. I only obeyed what I wanted to as she told me to do it. Even when I disappeared from human sight, I had to touch her first. I disappeared only when it was my desire to do so."

Cornelio's ultimate decision was in his own heart and within his own mind. No one could take that decision from him. He had strength within himself to say, "I will be what I want to be."

Man Is Responsible

I believe that any person who murders another person does so of his own volition and, therefore, must be held responsible for the things he does.

Though he may be infuriated with anger, it doesn't matter.

Though a sex spirit may rise up within him in an overwhelming way, he is still responsible – both to God and to man – for the deeds he commits.

We cannot overlook what God has said. He holds a person responsible for murder, so we must hold him responsible, too. If we will do that, we will certainly be what God would have us to be.

We can no longer allow ourselves and those around us to blame our actions on the devil. We can no longer use the excuse: "The devil made me do it!"

There are several factors that can be examined as reasons for unprovoked murder. In the chapters that follow, I will discuss perhaps the most prominent of them all: hostility, cultism, and sex.

11
Hostility and Unprovoked Murder

If you study the lives of people who commit murder, whether it be male or female, you will find that inside they are boiling with hostility. The ultimate result of hostility will be some form of demon possession.

In the Bible, hate and murder are classed together. First John 3:15 says, *Whosoever hateth his brother is a murderer: and ye know that no murderer hath eternal life abiding in him.*

If you hate your brother, you are a murderer and no murderer has eternal life. In other words, if you have hate in your heart, you have no way of ever going to heaven. Hate will cause your immortal soul to lose its position in heaven – the position God wants you to have.

A Spirit of Hate

Hate is a negative response of the inner person. It is like a disease, very much like cancer. It never stops eating until its victim is dead.

Once you begin to hate, the situation will not get better; it will only get worse. You will hate more next year than you hated this year.

Hate is an evil thing that eventually will lead to demon possession. You will find yourself hating one thing, then switching over and hating something else. You will be unable to stop hating because that spirit of hate inside you knows no termination except death.

Hate invariably demonstrates itself in the form of hostility, usually directed toward another human being. Oftentimes it will be directed toward the person you love and care for the most – your husband or wife, your children, your mother or father.

Sometimes it is directed toward a group, like an ethnic group – blacks, whites, Chinese, Mexicans, etc.

It could be directed toward police and government officials, or toward certain churches and religious groups.

Hate and Revenge

Eventually, this kind of hate will surpass human reasoning and ultimately cause a person to kill. The case of Theodore Streleski, detailed in chapter 2, is a prime example.

Streleski felt hostility toward his math professor, Dr. Karel De Leeuw. He viewed Dr. De Leeuw as opposition to his development. That feeling of hostility grew into hate, then developed into an overwhelming desire for revenge. He had to kill. In Streleski's mind, the professor was a hindrance that would have to be destroyed.

Our Lord Jesus Christ was hurt during His three years of ministry; but He had no revenge toward those who hurt Him, no hate toward those who nailed Him to the cross. If Theodore Streleski had met the right person, his life could have been happy.

All unprovoked murder has hostility at its roots.

If a person does not learn as a child to control his temper and pattern of negative thinking, he will, with time, learn to hate and even to murder.

No one kills without being angry at someone or something. Killers always hate. They see murder as a way of getting even with the human race. Murder is the climax and terminal point of hate.

Hostility Defined

The word "hostile" comes from the Latin *hostilis,* meaning "enemy." One dictionary defines it as "an unfriendly attitude; antagonism, opposition, or resistance in thought or principle." In reality, it is a deadly venom capable of robbing us of joy, peace, healthy relationships, and life itself.

Hostility is an emotional problem that can best be dealt with by the application of spiritual truths. Because it cripples human personalities and dwarfs the spirit and mind if not cleansed by confession and forgiveness, it soon spreads to contaminate all other emotions. What starts as a tiny germ of bitterness or anger can erupt into emotional instability and manifest itself in a variety of physical illnesses. Worst of all, it is highly contagious; a hostile person can cause others to become abrasive. This negative emotion passes from friend to friend, parent to child, teacher to student, and from governments to whole nations.

Hostility is one of Satan's most effective weapons, separating man from man and man from God. And no one is immune – not you, not me.

Two Sides of Anger

As beings created in the image of God, we have been instilled with a full spectrum of human emotions. Emotions can be either positive or negative. Too often, however, they are labeled as acceptable or unacceptable without understanding what triggered the feelings in the first place. Our capacity to experience emotions is one of God's most precious gifts; this was demonstrated in Christ's own personality. Anger is the emotion most often associated with hostility, yet anger is not always sinful.

The Bible shows us that God Himself, Who is the essence of love, is fully capable of anger. In the Old Testament alone the word "anger" appears over 450 times, and 375 of those references relate to God's anger.

According to author David Augsburger:

Conflict is neither good nor bad, right or wrong. Conflict simply is. How we view, approach, and work through our differences does – to a large extent – determine our whole life pattern.[1]

Ephesians 4:26 says, *Be ye angry, and sin not. . . ."* God understands the necessity of expressing, rather than repressing, feelings such as anger. It is partly the purpose of this book to help Christians deal with potentially destructive emotions in a biblical manner, *for it is out of the festering brew of unconfessed and unresolved hatred, anger, fear, and resentment that hostility is born.*

Let us then carefully define hostility *not* as the flash of emotion that comes in response to a painful or unpleasant situation, but rather as the result of harboring those feelings in an unforgiving attitude of resentment.

The last half of Ephesians 4:26 says, *. . . let not the sun go down upon your wrath.* This implies that one should resolve his differences with others and deal with his feelings of anger as soon as possible. Hostility becomes a problem when we allow our angry feelings to fester. Just as an infected wound left unattended can result in the development of gangrene, so unresolved hostility can become destructive and hinder our relations with others and with God Himself.

There is no virtue in clinging stubbornly to one's "rights." Hebrews 12:14 advises that we *follow peace with all men, and holiness, without which no man shall see the Lord,*

---

[1]David Augsburger, *Caring Enough To Confront* (Glendale, CA: Regal, 1973), p. 11.

and verse 15 explains why, cautioning, . . . *lest any root of bitterness springing up trouble you, and thereby many be defiled.*

Jesus spoke of the folly of being unwilling to give up one's hostile feelings. *For if ye forgive men their trespasses, your heavenly Father will also forgive you: But if ye forgive not men their trespasses, neither will your Father forgive your trespasses* (Matthew 6:14,15). Plainly, the consequences of hanging onto hostility are too great – we risk blocking God's forgiveness.

Where Are All the Hostile Humans?

In the deepest jungles of Africa, we see animals preying upon one another in order to survive. Yet hostility by our definition is not often found in the animal kingdom; rarely do we see an animal kill out of greed or for revenge. Only when he is hungry, wounded, frightened, or agitated does he become a hostile killer.

Unfortunately, this is not always true of people. Not only do we display hostility when we feel threatened by something or someone outside themselves, but we are fully capable of being moved to hostility by greed, hate, or revenge.

In more primitive areas of the world there exist whole tribes of hostile people whose culture is steeped in hatred, deceit, and distrust of anyone outside their immediate social group. A high capacity for rage and violence is considered a desirable trait and actually is encouraged.

But we cannot pretend that this kind of hostility is confined to the more isolated areas of the globe. Many people today live in emotional jungles of despair, discontent, and disappointment. Hostility is a living volcano of resentment erupting in our homes, our schools, and our cities. It infects the educated as well as the uneducated;

the rich as well as the poor. The young. The old. Believers and nonbelievers alike. It seeps its way into the hearts and minds of its most zealous opponents, turning the very body of Christ against itself. We cannot continue to hold this problem at arm's length, refusing to claim it as our own. Hostility is not just our neighbors' problem; it can be found in our own homes. It doesn't exist only in our enemies' hearts, but in our own also.

Human history is a study of hostility. Wars, revolutions, murders, deceit – rarely has the course of human events been altered drastically by anything but hostile means. The Bible is full of examples: Cain's hostility towards Abel; Esau's hostility towards Isaac; King Saul's towards David; the Pharisees' towards Jesus – all examples of hostility that changed the course of history.

Today our cities seethe with hostility. The Watts riots of the sixties and the 1980 racial violence in Florida stand out as tragic examples of the tremendous force of destruction released when the "volcano" finally erupts. But such demonstrations are only symptomatic of the inner rage and hostility of men and women we pass on the street, or go to school with, or work with each day.

Dr. Karl A. Menninger attributes the growing violence to the population explosion and crowded living conditions. He says that crowding people together aggravates tensions and causes irritations that make us more prone to violence.

Recently I was in New York City. A few blocks from my hotel I stopped a policeman to ask the quickest way back.

He looked at me sternly and said, "Sir, I am a policeman with a gun, and if I were going to your hotel I'd take a cab."

I blinked my eyes a couple of times and said, "I am out for a walk."

"No," he said, "you're out to die. This is New York." I took a cab.

Of course, all of us are aware of the dangers of walking in certain areas of our larger cities, but even the streets of small towns and the nicer residential areas are becoming unsafe. Our society has learned to live behind locked doors and barred windows. We glance nervously over our shoulders at the sound of hurried footsteps coming up behind us, even in broad daylight on a busy street; and we warn our children not to talk to strangers.

Our world is literally destroying itself through hostility. The very earth seems to be rebelling against the rape of its natural resources and the pollution of its air and water. We live in constant fear of nuclear war or economic disaster.

As Christians we view the growing hostility in the world from another perspective. Luke 21:9-28 warns of wars, commotions, nation fighting against nation, and the persecution and imprisonment of Christians. It speaks of Christian parents, brethren, kinfolks, and friends being betrayed and even put to death. Hatred will abound; these will be days of vengeance and distress among nations. Having been warned of all this, we are told, *When these things begin to come to pass, then look up, and lift up your heads; for your redemption draweth nigh* (Luke 21:28).

There is a message for humanity in this hostile age. "Wake up! Recognize where we are. The King is coming and the end of this world is near!"

Christians have a tremendous responsibility during these last days. We will soon witness the greatest explosion of naked, brutal hostility in the history of mankind.

12
What Causes Hostility?

Hostility is a spiritual affliction of the mind and heart. It is not inborn, as some would have us believe. Aggressionist Konrad Lorenz declares:

Aggression, in the proper and narrower sense of the word, is the fighting instinct in beast and man which is directed against members of the same species. It serves that species by balancing the distribution of its members over the available environment and by selecting the most rugged members to do the reproducing of the species.[1]

This view labels human beings as simply a more highly developed form of animal life, evolved from the ape and at the mercy of their baser instincts.

This is in direct contradiction to the biblical revelation that man was created uniquely in the image of God and was given dominion over the rest of creation. Certainly such a creature has the ability to control his own emotions and actions.

Hostility is not caused by a person's "hot Irish blood" or "fiery Latin temper." Cultural background cannot be blamed for an individual's lack of emotional discipline. No one is born hostile. Rather, children are born with a natural ability to vent their emotions in a healthy way, preventing the buildup of anger and frustration that leads

---

[1]Konrad Lorenz, *On Aggression,* Trans. Marjorie K. Wilson (New York: Bantam, 1970), n.p.

to hostility. That is why one moment they can be crying as if their hearts would break, and the next moment they are playing happily without a care in the world. They deal with each feeling as it comes.

Hostility's Roots

The roots of hostility cannot legitimately be traced to past hurts or disappointments. In his book, *Man and Aggression,* Ashley Montagu claims that the kind of behavior a person displays in any circumstance is determined largely by his past experiences. For unregenerate people, locked within the prison of their past sin and failure, this may be true. But when Jesus died on the cross and rose again, He broke our bondage to the past and freed every believer to make right choices in every area of our lives. Whether we do so or not is our own responsibility.

Sin, not nature, is the cause of hostility. It came first out of the pride of the angel Lucifer, who sought to exalt himself above God. Ezekiel 28:17 speaks of his pride and its consequences:

Thine heart was lifted up because of thy beauty, thou hast corrupted thy wisdom by reason of thy brightness: I will cast thee to the ground, I will lay thee before kings, that they may behold thee.

Hostility's Backbone

Pride is the backbone of hostility. Pride keeps us rigid – unwilling to bend until we see the other person broken, unwilling to forgive unless the other person confesses and seeks forgiveness, unwilling to forget until the situation is resolved and *we* have been justified. Pride can keep us from reaching out a conciliatory hand when we are wrong, and especially when we are right. More marriages fall victim to this kind of unwillingness to give than any other social or emotional problem.

A young pastor once shared with a group of husbands a discipline the Lord was working in his life. "No matter how wrong I think my wife is or how right I think I am, I know that after the storm is over I am to make the first move towards smoothing the troubled waters between us. I am the head of my household and must love my wife as Jesus loved the Church. To me that means dying to self enough to be the first one to say, 'I'm sorry.' By that, I am not always saying, 'I've changed my mind. You're right and I'm wrong,' but I am saying, 'I love you and I appreciate your feelings and am willing to talk things through.'"

Pride gives place to a myriad of other sins, such as selfish ambition, which was Lucifer's downfall:

> *How art thou fallen from heaven, O Lucifer, son of the morning! how art thou cut down to the ground, which didst weaken the nations!*
>
> *For thou hast said in thine heart, I will ascend into heaven, I will exalt my throne above the stars of God: I will sit also upon the mount of the congregation, in the sides of the north:*
>
> *I will ascend above the heights of the clouds; I will be like the most High.*
>
> Isaiah 14:12-14

Through Satan, sin and hostility were transmitted to a sinless earth and passed to Adam and Eve in the form of rebellion against God. Again, the selfish ambition to *be as gods, knowing good and evil* was the enticement (Genesis 3:5). Once sin entered the human race, it was passed from generation to generation, and hostility was born.

> *And the Lord God said unto the serpent, Because thou hast done this . . . I will put enmity between thee*

*and the woman, and between thy seed and her seed; it
shall bruise thy head, and thou shalt bruise his heel.*
Genesis 3:14,15

This hostility was to be between Eve's seed and
Satan, not between men. Satan takes this natural enmity
very seriously. He despises mankind and does everything
in his power to keep us from discovering the reality of
life in Jesus Christ. Failing that, he taunts, confuses,
tempts, and accuses, attacking any way he can to prevent
believers from fully understanding and effectively using
the spiritual weapons and authority that are theirs according to the Word of God and before which Satan cannot
stand.

Is it any wonder that hostility runs rampant across
the face of the earth?

Any number of negative feelings can lead to hostility.
The everyday tensions, pressures, and frustrations of
living in our fast-paced society provide a hothouse environment for emotional hostilities. Anxiety levels have
never been higher. Changing moral and social standards,
and the general lack of optimism in the world today have
provided people with a whole new set of worries and
fears. They feel themselves losing control of their lives.
Without the security of a personal relationship with One
who holds the future in His hand, people often feel they
are at the mercy of their circumstances. This unsettling
state of affairs sets them on edge, ready to release their
tension over the smallest offense.

Prayer Power

God has a different suggestion – prayer.

*Be careful for nothing; but in every thing by prayer
and supplication with thanksgiving let your requests
be made known unto God.*

And the peace of God, which passeth all understanding, shall keep your hearts and minds through Christ Jesus.

Philippians 4:6,7

A young man who was struggling with his Christian walk asked his grandfather, a dear saint of God, just how he managed not only to stay strong in his faith for over eighty years, but how he did so with such obvious joy and peace.

"I've never seen you angry or irritable or even discouraged. What's your secret?" the grandson asked.

"It's simple," replied the old man, with a smile. "Each morning I wake up early and get on my knees in prayer. And I don't get up until I feel His wonderful joy and peace flood my heart. Then I know I am ready to face whatever the day may bring."

Few of us have that kind of unruffled demeanor. And few of us see that kind of an even-keeled disposition in those around us. Why not? Without doubt it relates to the time we invest in equipping ourselves to face the enemy's onslaughts.

Prayer is a key. Power to stand up to whatever the day may bring can come as we saturate our minds with the joy of the Lord. As we spend time in unbroken communion with Him – through prayer and reading the Bible – we will find ourselves better able to face whatever comes our way. It may sound simplistic, but it is a proven method of doing combat with our adversary, the devil.

Competition

Competitiveness – in business, on a social level, in school, sports, and politics – can result in deep-seated hostility if it is not carefully identified and dealt with. We in the United States have been brought up to believe that the best man always wins; so if we don't win or at least make a showing close to the top, we take it as a commentary on our worth. This stirs up feelings of insecurity and inferiority, two more key roots of hostility.

It has been observed that to a great degree the amount of hostility produced in an individual is directly related to his feelings of inferiority at the time. It is much easier to be kind, sympathetic, and unselfish after accomplishment than after failure.

Not everyone achieves in ways that are recognized by society. Sometimes accomplishment seems to evade all but extremely gifted individuals. But the failure to recognize real accomplishment lies in our definition of what achievement is. We are too narrow in our thinking. A mother may be as accomplished in her role of soothing a troubled child as her husband is in negotiating a big contract for the company that employs him. But too often the mother feels frustrated and inferior and comes to the end of a busy day with hostile feelings, ready to explode.

The consequences of excessive feelings of inferiority are graphically illustrated in the rise and fall of Adolf Hitler. It was because of the crushing defeat and humiliating reparations of World War I that the German people were so susceptible to a leader who stood for superiority and hatred.

Our Hostile Children

Parents can be a prime source of hostility in their children. A lack of trust and affirmation in the home can produce a growing snowball of anger and frustration within a child. If this is not melted by the warmth of honest communication and expressions of love, it can freeze parents and child into positions of constant confrontation.

Recently, a well-known television performer talked

about his relationship with his pastor-father. He talked with great admiration about his father's powerful pulpit ministry. His father's preaching exuded the love of God, and many souls were saved.

"Then," the man went on, "he would step down from the pulpit, take me by the hand, and we would go home. Just like that, my father would change from the living expression of love and concern he was to the congregation, to an aloof, undemonstrative man who never once put his arms around me and told me he loved me."

My heart went out to that young man as the camera closed in on his tortured expression. "I never have been able to understand how God could love me when my father didn't," he confessed.

Sibling rivalry is another painful result of parents not being sensitive to their children's needs and feelings. There is nothing more painful for a child than the feeling that he is less loved and appreciated than his brother or sister.

The story of Joseph and his brothers is a classic illustration of this problem. Angry and hurt that their father loved Joseph more than he loved them and openly favored him, his brothers sold Joseph into slavery, telling their father that he had been killed.

Many children are constantly trying to live up to the accomplishments of older brothers and sisters. Some feel pushed aside emotionally when a new baby comes into the family. Their pain and hostility may be equal to or even greater than Joseph's brothers' and will probably leave scars that they will carry into their adult lives and relationships.

The outside world is going to do enough emotional damage to children who aren't quite as bright, talented, or attractive as their siblings; the home should be a place where their self-worth is reinforced, where they know they are loved and accepted just as they are.

The unending pressure of meeting a child's physical and emotional needs can produce another form of hostility. Most parents battle this in silence, ashamed that they are capable of feeling such strong negative emotions toward their own children. I could read the distress and guilt on one young mother's face as she sat in my office and described her experience.

Nancy was an attractive, intelligent, basically happy mother of three small children, ages one, three, and five. She and Bill wanted to have their children two years apart, as they felt it would be nice for the children to play together and that it would give the family a sense of unity.

Normally Nancy copes with the constant demands of her offspring with good humor and loving patience, but one day was an exception. The house, which was usually kept in reasonable order, reflected her mood. Beds were unmade, dishes were stacked in the sink, and toys were scattered from one end of the house to the other.

Nancy viewed the scene with fatalistic pessimism. The idea of making one bed or washing one dish overwhelmed her. Her body felt drained of all energy, and her nerves were raw and sensitive. From the moment she woke up she knew it was going to be "one of those days," and she was right.

The children immediately picked up on Nancy's depression and (as small children seem to do) responded by becoming whiney and even more demanding than usual. The house was filled with the sound of their shrill little screams and shouts of "Mommy, Billy pulled my hair" or "Mommy, I had the toy first and Susie won't give it back."

Irritating as the constant noise was, it was the quiet lulls in between that demanded immediate investigation. Children are rarely quiet unless they have found something fascinating to do, like trying on Mommy's makeup or sampling the pretty "candy" in the medicine cabinet.

Nancy found herself walking an emotional tightrope. Her irritation grew with each additional crisis and demand, threatening to push her off balance. The intensity of her emotions was frightening, but she felt helpless before them.

At lunchtime, the kids were at the table arguing over who would get the last cookie. The baby was in his high chair playing "drop-the-spoon-and-watch-Mommy-pick-it-up." Just as the phone rang, Billy made a grab for the cookie and knocked over his milk, drenching Susie's lap. Susie broke out into gasping sobs, while the baby decided to add his lunch to the mess on the floor.

Something inside Nancy's head snapped. She felt a definite sensation of losing control. Trembling with rage, she grabbed Billy by the arm and swung him out of the chair. "Get a towel and clean this milk up! Susie, stop your sniveling. I can't stand it! And you," she rasped through clenched teeth at the baby, who by this time was loudly voicing his complaints, "I'm not going to pick up this mess one more time! I want you all to go to your rooms and not come out till I say so! Move it! Now!"

The room fell into silence. Nancy stood frozen in place, her face in her hands. An overwhelming sense of guilt and failure flooded over her, replacing the anger and bringing the emotional release of tears.

"Oh, Lord Jesus, help me! Only You know how close I am to hitting them. If I had started, I don't know if I would have been able to stop. You know how much I love my children . . . but at that moment I felt such anger and resentment. Oh, God, help me. Please help!"

Every mother can relate to Nancy's situation, for what parent hasn't faced moments when the demands of the family seem more than he or she can handle?

Unfortunately, some parents are not able to resist the temptation to vent their suppressed hostility on their children. I am sure no parent sets out to purposely hurt his child, but as Nancy said, once you start it's hard to stop. Nearly ten million child abuse cases come before our courts each year. Thousands of children are literally beaten to death, victims of their parents' misdirected and uncontrolled hostility. Countless others survive, physically and emotionally damaged for life. Most will probably inflict their own pain and rage on their friends, their mates, and later on their own children.

Hostility has infected the home in other ways. Statistics indicate that one out of four families in the United States is touched by incest. You would be amazed at the number of women who write or come to me with similar stories. "Brother Sumrall, the first person who ever sexually attacked me was my father. He would send my mother out for something, just so he could lay with me. He told me he would kill me if I told. Now I have a husband and children of my own, and I am still so angry inside!"

Ephesians 6:4 says, *Ye fathers, provoke not your children to wrath: but bring them up in the nurture and admonition of the Lord.*

Keith Miller tells the touching story of a former pro athlete who finally got tired of rebelling against God and decided to make an all-out commitment to Jesus. Almost immediately, his family saw him change from a hostile, belligerent tyrant to a man who honestly wanted to love and take care of them. He began spending time with his children and openly communicating with his wife.

About two weeks later his twelve-year-old son came in to talk to him. This boy had no friends at school and had begun to steal things from around the neighborhood to get attention. He was almost totally alone. "Dad," he said hesitantly, "what's happened to you lately?" His dad (who had been a tough professional athlete) looked up from his desk. "Well, son," he struggled for the right words, "I – guess I was making a pretty big mess out of my life and I decided I'd ask God to take over and show me how to live it."

The boy looked at him and then down at the floor. "Dad," he said quietly, "I think I'd like to do that too."

The father just stood there with tears running down his cheeks and he and the boy held each other and wept together. The next day Jack had to go to New York on a business trip for two weeks. On the way back he was anxious to get home. When his plane got in, his son broke through the crowd and ran out on the ramp to meet his father. His eyes were shining with excitement! Hugging him, he said breathlessly, in a kind of grateful wonder, "Daddy, do you know what God has done?"

"No, what son?" his dad asked.

"He's changed every kid in my class!!"[2]

Children model themselves after the examples we set before them. The home is the perfect place for children to learn to handle their feelings in a healthy way – to learn gentleness, kindness, forgiveness, and unselfishness. It is also where the opposite is easily learned.

I was sitting on the front porch of a pastor's home one afternoon, and a sweet-faced little neighbor girl of five or six came over and sat down with me. She looked up at

---

[2]Keith Miller, *A Second Touch* (Waco, TX: Word, 1967), p. 156.

me and said in a matter-of-fact voice, "I'm going to kill you."

I reacted as though she had said she was going to kiss me. "That's very sweet of you. Who did you hear say that?"

"That's what my daddy told my mama a while ago," she replied.

"Yes," I sighed, "that's what I thought."

It is by such careless words that seeds of hostility are sown into the fertile soil of our children's minds and hearts. How easily are the sins of a parent perpetuated in his child!

It is a foolish person who transmits hostility from generation to generation.

Jealousy and Hostility

Jealousy has been called a "green-eyed monster," and rightly so. It is an insidious thing, born out of our discontentment with who we are or what we have.

A very good friend of mine said that a Christian competitor of his was doing so well with his business that he found it difficult to speak peaceably about him when anyone mentioned his name. They were both building contractors, and one was building more houses than the other.

My friend finally prayed, "Lord, I don't dislike this man. We are friends. We belong to the same clubs and attend the same church. But every time his name is mentioned I say something negative about him. I don't like it in myself, and I want to quit."

"Do you?" the Lord gently challenged.

"Yes, I really do," my friend answered.

"All right," the Lord said. "Every time you say something negative about him, send him a twenty-five-dollar check as a gift."

You would be amazed at how quickly my friend learned to say good things about that gentleman when it was costing him twenty-five dollars every time he let his jealousy control his tongue.

Proverbs 10:12 says, *Hatred stirreth up strifes: but love covereth all sins.*

Hatred and resentment are common producers of hostility. There is nothing more difficult for most people than forgiving someone who has hurt or persecuted them. And yet we have only to look at the lives and attitudes of saints such as Corrie ten Boom, who have been the objects of naked, unrestrained brutality, to see that forgiveness is possible through the power of God.

John Perkins, the founder of Voice of Calvary Ministries, was another such victim of blind hate and prejudice. As a black pastor in Mississippi in the late 1960s and early 1970s, he felt called to speak out in favor of the civil rights movement that was sweeping through the South, triggering fear and hostility in those who resented the inevitable changes. As a result, Perkins was put in jail and nearly beaten to death. The following is part of the testimony of a fellow victim:

[The sheriffs] had a leather blackjack thing and they began beating on Reverend Brown, Reverend Perkins, David Nall, and myself . . . they beat Rev. Brown down to the floor and then Rev. Perkins was dragged over on the other side and beaten down by about five other officers. I could hear them being beaten and then I was knocked out and when I came to I heard them ordering Rev. Perkins to mop up the blood that was on the floor and Rev. Perkins was lying sorta stunned on the floor and they kicked him until he got up. . . . Then Sheriff E. and two or three patrol officers would walk by every two or three minutes and kick or hit Rev. Perkins with one of their blackjacks or their feet.[3] Most of us find it impossible to understand the intensity of hatred and disregard for human dignity that allows such violence. It is even more inconceivable that someone could live through such an ordeal without coming away bitter and full of anger. But here again, God's power protected a man from being infected by the hate and hostility of those who persecuted him. Perkins concludes the retelling of the nightmare.

They were like savages – like some horror out of the night. And I can't forget their faces, so twisted with hate. It was like looking at white-faced demons. Hate did that to them.

But you know, I couldn't hate back. When I saw what hate had done to them, I couldn't hate back. I could only pity them. I didn't ever want hate to do to me what it had done to those men.[4]

The potential destructive power of bitterness and the hate that is its direct descendant is greater than any other negative human emotion. And God will not tolerate it in His children. Dr. Jack Hayford explains:

God refuses to raise a breed of sons and daughters who are unlike Him. He has sired us. He insists that every latent trait of our former heritage, as offspring of Adam's race, be wormed out of us. He won't allow unforgiveness to continue. It's not in His nature, so He confronts it in ours.[5]

---

[3]John Perkins, *Let Justice Roll Down* (Glendale, CA: Regal, 1976), p. 163.
[4]Ibid., pp. 163,165.
[5]Dr. Jack Hayford, *Prayer Is Invading the Impossible* (Plainfield, NJ: Logos, 1977), p. 103.

Hostility and Prejudice

Fear, misunderstanding, and ignorance often create hostility and another closely related feeling – prejudice. In the jungles of Ecuador a few years ago, a group of missionaries were murdered by a tribe of Indians who had been convinced by their leader that the white-skinned outsiders were a threat. Racial and language barriers prevented communication that could have explained the missionaries' presence and put the tribesmen's fear to rest.

Some time later, the message of the gospel was preached to these people, and many responded. Today, many of these Indians serve the Lord by spreading the good news to others who still live in the darkness of their ignorance and fear.

Fear and Misunderstanding

Fear and misunderstanding produce a vicious cycle. What we don't understand, we fear; what we fear, we don't take time to understand.

Lack of self-esteem leaves one vulnerable to anger and hostility. A person who can express his anger in a positive, thoughtful way likes himself better than someone who hurts himself or others. A low self-image also makes one more sensitive to criticism, more easily hurt or angered.

Fear of rejection causes a hostile reaction. When we feel rejected, we in turn reject others. Being ignored as though we don't exist or being treated as though we are worthless can produce an instinctive, spontaneous reaction of anger. In this instance, the anger is a demand that our value as people be recognized.

Feelings of uselessness or of not being wanted or needed can produce deep hostility. This is a common problem among the elderly, who are often forced to retire not only from their jobs but also from active participation in other areas as well. Many become cranky and irritable, driving people away, when what they want and need is to be accepted back into the ranks of responsible adults who have something of value to contribute.

Dependency, or the fear of becoming dependent upon a person or a relationship, can illicit angry, hostile behavior. Many people today have become obsessed with false concepts of freedom, individuality, and self-gratification that twenty years ago would have been more rightly labeled irresponsibility, self-centeredness, and selfishness. This concern for "me, myself, and I" has spawned a growing disdain for commitment in relationships. People don't want to get involved because involvement costs. "Noninvolvement, however, creates an emptiness and hostility that are much harder to handle," writes Elizabeth Skoglund in her book, *To Anger, With Love.*[6]

Besides the frustration and anger created by fluctuating social values many people also experience inner hostility that is derived from a sense of rootlessness. This is partially the result of value conflict, but it is also due to the increased isolation of the individual in our society (and this affects Christians too). . . .

Perhaps a feeling of meaninglessness is related to all the reasons for anger in our society. An increasing number of people seek psychological help because they are bored. Many of the very young feel an apathy toward life that promotes feelings of hostility as well as destructive behavior. . . . Extremes of individualism contribute to

---

[6]Elizabeth R. Skoglund, *To Anger, With Love* (New York: Harper & Row, 1977), p. 21.

boredom because meaning can be found only in [committed] relationships. Value changes and rootlessness make a person wonder what life is all about, and even the Christian, who is sure of his or her eternal destiny, may question the how and why of now.[7]

Resentment's Poison

Resentment and bitterness go hand in hand with hostility. When we resent a painful or difficult happening in our lives, such as the death of a loved one or a sickness or the loss of a job, we soon find ourselves growing bitter, no longer able to take pleasure in all the good things God has blessed us with. We strike out at family and friends, unaware of the way bitterness has poisoned our thinking and relationships.

The resentful person stands to be hurt the most by nursing his grudge. As we relive in our thinking whatever it was that caused us to become hostile, we allow the poison of these undesirable feelings to endanger even our health. Many physical problems that have no physiological cause are directly related to what is going on in our heads – unresolved problems, anger, and hurts (real or imagined).

We need to read and reread First Corinthians 13 often. In verse 5 we are told that love *doth not behave itself unseemly, seeketh not her own, is not easily provoked, thinketh no evil.*

How we need to learn these godly principles and make them a part of our everyday experience! What grief and anguish we would spare ourselves if we consciously practiced these admonitions meant for our own good!

---

[7]Ibid., pp. 19,21.

Resentment usually gives way to vengeance, as we plot ways to get even with someone we feel has wronged us. How quickly we forget Romans 12:19: *Avenge not yourselves, but rather give place unto wrath: for it is written, Vengeance is mine; I will repay, saith the Lord.*

What is the answer for the person who struggles with resentment and bitterness? The counsel of the Word stands sure:

> *Let all bitterness, and wrath, and anger, and clamour, and evil speaking, be put away from you, with all malice: And be kind one to another, tenderhearted, forgiving one another, even as God for Christ's sake hath forgiven you.*
>
> Ephesians 4:31,32

We must guard our thought lives. Philippians 4:8 lists preventive measures the Christian can employ:

> *Finally, brethren, whatsoever things are true, whatsoever things are honest, whatsoever things are just, whatsoever things are pure, whatsoever things are lovely, whatsoever things are of good report; if there be any virtue, and if there be any praise, think on these things.*

The promise is that if we do this, the God of peace will be with us. (See v. 9.)

Recently some friends traveled from Michigan to Indiana to hear me speak. I was surprised and pleased to see them in the congregation, until they came up to speak to me after the service. They explained that they had come to confess the great bitterness and hostility they had felt for me and to ask my forgiveness.

I smiled in amazement. "That's a real revelation to me. I always thought you were some of my best friends!"

"No, we have not been your friends," they replied. "We have spoken badly about you behind your back."

I forgave them, and they left with peace restored to their hearts. To this day I do not know what caused such deep bitterness in those people, but I learned long ago the wisdom of not reacting to another's pain and weakness out of my own.

There is a story about John Wesley walking down a path and meeting a man who hated him because of his preaching. The man stood astride of the walk, saying, "I won't get out of the way for a fool."

John Wesley stepped aside. "Sir, I will," he said, letting the man pass. We must refuse to be a part of another person's hostility.

Hostile Humor

We must also be careful how we speak to other people. Hostile teasing or belittling can generate tremendous hostility. This is particularly a problem between husbands and wives. It is often tempting to point out an irritating flaw by way of a teasing remark, or to retaliate for past hurts by making a spouse look foolish in front of others.

One time I was in Alaska, staying in the home of a man who had gone there in search of gold. He had found an Eskimo wife, and had become the town's postmaster.

They had a quarrel. She said something in broken English and he responded with, "*Squaw,* you shut up!"

Her immediate shame and embarrassment were painfully obvious. He had deliberately belittled her in front of us by calling her a squaw instead of his wife. I still chuckle when I picture the infuriated little Eskimo woman's retort: "White woman good enough for you. Eskimo woman *too* good!"

When you belittle a person you attack the most vulnerable, intimate part of his psyche – his sense of self-worth. Hostility is an inevitable result.

Finally, sin and feelings of conviction over sin in one's life can cause tremendous hostility. A Chicago newspaper reported the story of a Christian father who went to see his son in prison. Heartbroken over his son's condition, the man asked him to give his heart to Jesus. Before the prison guards could stop him, the boy had beaten his father to the ground with his fists and walked off cursing. The son was under conviction for his sins and he vented the resulting hostility upon his godly father, who wanted to see him saved and released from his terrible bondage of guilt.

Sadly, hostility hurts no one more than those who allow it to take root in their lives.

Anger Towards God and His People

We must recognize that Satan's main strategy is to divide and conquer. Jesus said that every kingdom divided against itself is brought to desolation and that *every city or house divided against itself shall not stand* (Matthew 12:25).

Hostility against God's children robs us of strength and leaves us far more vulnerable to deception and spiritual attack then we would be if the circle of fellowship were unbroken.

A friend relates the story of Stonewall Jackson, who saw his men fighting among themselves over battle strategy. The general is said to have jumped into the argument, stating, "Remember, gentlemen, the enemy is over there," pointing in the direction of the battle. Likewise, how tragic it is for church members to fight each other while Satan gains victories over men's immortal souls.[8]

---

[8]Helen Hosier, *It Feels Good To Forgive* (Irvine, CA: Harvest House, 1979), p. 61.

Then, there are Christians who are angry with God. We are never supposed to be angry with God. If we are, He may strike us down with a bolt of lightning or turn us into a pillar of salt! In reality, the Bible gives us a graphic illustration that seems to indicate *the exact opposite.*

We are familiar with the story of the Prophet Jonah who rebelled against God's direction for his life. (God wanted him to warn the people of Nineveh of His imminent judgment and destruction unless they repented from their evil ways.) Jonah's disobedience caused him to end up in the belly of a big fish. After three days God caused the fish to vomit Jonah up onto dry land, and Jonah, who had experienced a decided change of heart, headed straight for Nineveh to deliver God's message. The result was a great spiritual revival as the entire city confessed its sin and sought God's mercy and forgiveness. And God spared them.

But instead of being overjoyed by the people's honest repentance, the Bible says that Jonah was displeased and very angry. (See Jonah 4:2-4.)

God was chiding Jonah for his selfish self-absorption, but there is nothing in His response to indicate that He was outraged by Jonah's uninhibited expression of his true feelings. Even as Jonah sat complaining and feeling sorry for himself God took pity on him, arranging for a vine to spring up and spread its leaves to shade him.

To think we can hide our anger from God by pretending it doesn't exist is ridiculous. We may be able to fool ourselves, but we can never fool Him. When something happens that hurts us deeply, we may direct our anger at the person or thing that hurt us. But underneath that hurt is the thought that since God is ultimately in control of everything, He *could* have done something to protect us.

In her book, *The Hidden Riches of Secret Places,* Hazel McAlister writes with soul-level honesty about her anger with God for letting her father die when she was fifteen.

I buried my anger. It was buried so deep that eventually I forgot about it. I didn't even know it was there.

Someone said, "We bury our feelings and they grow." Silently, stealthily, completely unknown to me, my anger grew. It colored everything I thought – especially spiritual things. It governed many of the things I did and caused me to make most of my mistakes.

I know now that to be angry is to be disobedient. The natural outgrowth of disobedience is rebellion, and with rebellion comes an unclean heart, a wrong spirit, and ultimately more anger.[9]

Hazel learned the importance of being honest with God about her feelings – not for His benefit but for her own. It is only by our willingness to take those hidden negative feelings and hurts out of the darkness and expose them, ugly and painful as they may be, that true healing and redemption can take place.

Even though God knows everything, we must talk to Him about the things that bother us in our hearts, and as we converse . . . with Him, we free Him to forgive our anger, our resentment, our bitterness, our self-imposed guilt, our attitudes, and our actions. They are all changed by the blood of His Son. God allows different experiences to come into our lives to discipline us, to mold us, to make us, and to shape us into His likeness.[10]

---

[9]Hazel McAlister, *The Hidden Riches of Secret Places* (Nashville, TN: Thomas Nelson, 1980), p. 28.
[10]Ibid., pp. 29,30.

While it is true that God is all-knowing, still *we* must articulate our hurts and whatever it is that is contributing to our hostility. When we feel that God is dealing with us harshly, we would do well to remember that God disciplines us as sons. (See Hebrews 12:7.) And although present chastening (problems, hurts, and anxieties) is not joyous, the promise is that *afterward it yieldeth the peaceable fruit of righteousness* (Hebrews 12:11). This peace is exactly the opposite of the hostility so often harbored in the human heart.

13
The Effects of Hostility

Our world is destroying itself through hostility. Wars ravage the land and kill the innocent. Racism fills our hearts with blind hate and turns neighbor against neighbor. The world's religions continue their contest for control of men's hearts and minds, while we in the body of Christ are robbed of our strength of unity by our own internal bickering.

Hostility eats away at the foundations of relationships, businesses, governments, and whole civilizations. Some historians believe that the great city of Athens, which dominated the world intellectually for hundreds of years, died internally from hostility. Everybody was angry at somebody. Everybody was suing somebody. The army couldn't win a battle because they were too busy fighting each other to fight the enemy effectively. By the time they were conquered, the Athenians were nearly unconscious from internal feuding. They had literally destroyed themselves before the enemy ever attacked.

America today is in a frighteningly similar situation. We're so full of hostility towards one another that it takes a terrible tragedy or serious threat to remind us that we must stand and work together to survive. We need one another, both individually and collectively, and if we don't determine to put our differences aside and reverse the deteriorating effects of hostility in our land, our society may suffer the same ending Athens did.

Irrational Hostility

Our court systems are booked years in advance, not only with criminal cases but with the petty grievances of friends and even family members who will not forgive and forget.

I read in the newspaper about two friends who were playing tennis together. One of them was inadvertently hit by the ball and received a black eye. Outraged, he took his opponent to court. The judge dismissed the case, saying, "You cannot sue a man for hitting a ball you happened to get in the way of."

The hearing of nonsensical cases such as this one costs taxpayers thousands of dollars each year. Worse, it keeps our courts from settling far more important problems in a timely manner.

Hostility has a crippling effect on the human personality. Joy, peace of mind, contentment, and rational thinking are replaced by hatred, vindictive thoughts, discontentment, and a general confusion. The Hebrew Talmud says, "As a man gets angry, he falls into error." Hostility clouds our thinking and leaves us vulnerable to all sorts of erroneous teachings and ideas.

Demonic Deception

The most reasonable of men becomes unpredictable and even dangerous in the grip of hostile emotions. His whole personality may change radically. He may be soft-spoken and apparently in control of his actions one moment, cruel, violent, and vindictive the next. Wife-beating, child abuse, and other acts of violence are generally the result of uncontrolled hostility.

When the full force of that emotional negativism is directed toward oneself, it gradually destroys the essential element of hope within the human heart, eating away at natural instincts of self-preservation, until suicide seems to offer a blessed relief from a life of pain and unresolved problems.

"It has been said that suicide is Satan's gateway to defeat, but Christ is the only Door to freedom and victory, "[1] writes Helen Hosier. According to her book, *Suicide, A Cry for Help,* suicide is the second leading cause of death among young people between the ages of fifteen and twenty-four. But it also takes its tragic toll on children as young as six and seven years old, on the middle-aged, and on the elderly. Neither money, fame, nor success can immunize us from an inner sense of worthlessness and helplessness that produces despair.

Paul said that unless a person receives help from others that can instill some hope within him, he may be *swallowed up with overmuch sorrow* (2 Corinthians 2:7).

Unless we are willing to do this, Satan will get the advantage. Those are not my words; again they come from Paul. (2 Corinthians 2:11.) Bitterness and discouragement can so overtake one that unless we who are strong in the Lord and aware of the adversary's tactics and come to the rescue of one who is overburdened with life's complexities, there is great danger that such a person will not recover, but will succumb to despair. It is in these moments that mental derangement can take over to the extent that even a committed Christian can commit suicide.

The final act of suicide is basically a resolution, a movement, perceived as the only possible way out of a life situation felt to be unbearable

---

[1]Helen Hosier, *Suicide, A Cry for Help* (Irvine, CA: Harvest House, 1978), p. 89.

by one of low sense of competence, with hope extinguished.[2]

Hostility opens the door to the most demonic kind of deception, and often blinds us to the simplest truths.

Habitual Hostility

Hostility destroys human potential and hinders productivity. The habitually hostile person is hard to teach, to work with, or to live with. His anger constantly gets in the way of personal growth, causing him to be impatient and less careful than he might otherwise be. Automobile accidents are often the result of drivers allowing their anger to take control of their steering wheels. And studies show that 80 to 90 percent of industrial accidents happen to only 10 percent of the workers. This is generally not attributed to a lack of skill on the job, but to a characteristic of aggression in certain personalities.

Although there is no doubt that hostility generates a certain amount of energy, it is usually an undisciplined energy that hinders more than helps. For this reason, professional athletes have learned to manifest less hostility than amateurs might show. Experience has taught them that hostility toward opponents or teammates usually ends in unnecessary errors.

Hostility puts people in prisons, hospitals, and insane asylums. It confuses issues, making it difficult to keep priorities in a healthy order.

The suppressed anger and hurt that lead to hostility tear families apart and destroy friendships by short-circuiting communication. Alan Loy McGinnis observes this in his book, *The Friendship Factor.*

When passively hostile people blow, their expression of anger is disproportionate to the complaint because they

---

[2]Ibid., p. 91.

are really ventilating a lot of past grievances all at once. The result is that communication shorts out.[3]

The Robber

Hostility isolates people in a world of "self." Since the one relating to a hostile person never knows when the wrong word or look is going to illicit a violent or cutting response, openness and honesty in the relationship are gradually replaced by a spirit of fear.

In a wider sense, this spirit of fear hangs like a pall over the earth, keeping us on guard and slightly uneasy whenever we're in unfamiliar territory. No longer do we assume the best of people. Instead, we expect the worst, and anything else is a pleasant surprise! No longer do we face the world with positive expectation and trust, but with skepticism and a "prove-it-to-me" attitude. Hostility takes away our spontaneity and places limitations on our human potential. It is a robber.

Hostility has invaded the classroom, making it difficult for our children to obtain a good education.

Dr. Kenneth L. Fish found rebellion and hostility in the schools so disturbing that he did extensive research in this area. His book, *Conflict and Dissent in the High School,* makes this statement:

> High school walkouts, sit-ins, and school closings . . . interfere with the regular course of learning; they complicate the already critical job of staffing schools with good teachers, and they are one more symptom of the disintegrative processes which threaten American society.[4]

---

[3]Alan Loy McGinnis, *The Friendship Factor* (Minneapolis, MN: Augsburg, 1979), p. 130.
[4]Kenneth L. Fish, *Conflict and Dissent in the High School* (New York: Bruce Publishing Co., 1970), p. 1.

It has also been observed that learning difficulties are seldom due to lack of intelligence. Often, a child's hostility toward his teacher stifles his motivation to learn. This was true of Albert Einstein. His schoolwork was so poor that his teachers and parents feared he was retarded. The headmaster of his school is quoted as saying, "He'll never make a success at anything!" However, it was hostile defiance against his teachers, not lack of ability, that caused Einstein's poor grades.

Young people's rebellion against authority has unfortunately caused more damage than a few failing grades. Dr. Milton Layden observes in *Escaping the Hostility Trap* that drug abuse is also directly linked to hostility.

> The principal reason a youngster starts taking drugs is his hostile feeling toward established authority. In a study involving hundreds of high school students, more of those who were exposed to drug information (its negative effects) became users than those who were not given any information at all. When an authority-hating youngster is warned of the dire consequences of drug abuse, he may start taking the drug as a means of defiance.[5]

It is also a proven fact that hostility is responsible for a number of other physical and emotional illnesses, such as insomnia, ulcers, headaches, heart attacks, obesity, alcoholism, gambling, infidelity, fatigue, hypertension, and nervous breakdowns.

---

[5]Dr. Milton Layden, *Escaping the Hostility Trap* (Englewood Cliffs, NJ: Prentice-Hall, 1977), p. 136.

14
Hostility and Soundness of Mind

Hostility does not spring full grown out of nowhere to suddenly take control of our lives. It begins as a seed of anger, resentment, or bitterness planted in the inner recesses of our minds. If not weeded out, it takes root and draws nourishment from undisciplined thoughts, negative attitudes, and other sin in our lives. Soon it becomes a motivating force, warping our logic, influencing our actions, and dictating our responses to others.

The Real Battle

Proverbs 23:7 says, *For as he thinketh in his heart, so is he: Eat and drink, saith he to thee; but his heart is not with thee.*

Our heart attitude and thought life are very closely related. What a man thinks in his heart determines what he is. Therefore, although our battle against hostility is a spiritual one, the battleground is the mind and the weapons are ideas and thoughts.

Having made peace through the blood of his cross, by him to reconcile all things unto himself; by him, I say, whether they be things in earth, or things in heaven.

And you, that were sometime alienated and enemies in your mind by wicked works, yet now hath he reconciled.

Colossians 1:20,21

Since the mind is the key to the personality, there is a continuous battle going on for control of our thought lives. We are constantly exposed to the subtle campaign

131

of the enemy through certain movies, television shows, magazines, books, and music that portray ungodly and hostile behavior as natural and healthy. Sin and perversion have been redefined and reclassified as "personal freedoms," and we are accused of having closed minds and being bigots if we dare call sin "sin."

In Romans 8:7 we are told that *the carnal mind is enmity against God...*, and First Peter 1:13 urges believers to *gird up the loins of your mind...* against the propaganda of unrighteousness.

Philippians 2:5 instructs us to *let this mind be in you, which was also in Christ Jesus.* This mental transformation cannot take place if our relationship with Christ only includes attending church on Sunday and saying "grace" at mealtimes. We must spend time getting to know Him through His Word and through meaningful conversations in prayer.

It is also a fact of life that we are influenced by our environment. Our friends and families have a tremendous influence upon our attitudes and thinking. Peer pressure is especially hard for the young to resist. I know from experience.

I grew up angry. I can't tell you why. I had a good home, and I believe God gave me a good mind. But I was caught up in a spirit of rebellion that dominated all my close friends. We fed one another's anger and dissatisfaction and shaped one another's thoughts to conform to our own hostility. I was a rebel on my way into an eternity without God.

Then I contracted tuberculosis. It was the best thing that could have happened to me. I lay in bed for five months, and not once did the gang come to see me. I realized how shallow and meaningless our relationships were and how confused my thinking had been.

When I was finally up and around again, my friends

suddenly reappeared, wanting to pick up where we had left off. "No," I told them, "you didn't want to see me when I was sick. I don't want to see you now that I'm well." I was finally free to think my own thoughts and make my own decisions.

Interpersonal Relationships

If our minds tell us we are not being treated as well as someone else, or that someone else is more talented or capable, we are open to resentment, envy, or feelings of inadequacy – all of which can lead to hostility.

The mind is constantly evaluating other people's behavior as acceptable or unacceptable, and we respond accordingly. This is how we often get into trouble. Since we cannot possibly read another's mind or heart we cannot know their needs or problems. Thus we make judgments based upon appearances, not fact.

My wife went to the post office one day to pick up our office mail. She greeted the postal clerk with a cheerful, "Good morning. How are you today?"

He just grunted.

The next day she returned and was helped by the same man. Again she greeted him with, "Good morning. It's a beautiful day, isn't it? How are you?"

No response.

The third morning the man was again sullen and unfriendly, and my wife began praying for him. By Friday she walked into the post office determined to be friendly, in spite of what she now considered the man's ungracious and unfriendly attitude. Instead, before she could say a word, the clerk leaned across the counter and said in a broken voice, "Mrs. Sumrall, I am sorry for the way I've behaved these last few days, but my wife died two weeks ago and I just can't get over it. I am the saddest person in the world."

Immediately my wife saw that it wasn't this man's nature to be surly and unpleasant. He had received a crushing blow and was still staggering from its impact. His attitude reflected his misery, and her conclusions about his personality had been mistaken.

So often it is the pain in us reacting to the pain in someone else that creates hostility. If we could only withhold judgment and table our response until we are sure we have the whole picture, a lot of unnecessary hurt and anger could be avoided. Instead, the human mind calls for immediate sympathy and understanding, and when it doesn't get it, it often strikes back without thinking things through or trying to see the other person's point of view.

Our thinking is also influenced by associations. The mind links a current situation with something from the past and draws a conclusion that can be completely erroneous and misleading.

A few years ago I traveled into the Grand Chaco Boreano in Paraguay. We went by river as far as the boat could take us, then traveled by horseback for several miles. When we reached the area where the most primitive Indians lived, my interpreter said to me, "I must warn you not to use the word 'Christian' around these people. They might cut your throat."

Astounded, I asked him why.

He explained that the Paraguayan army had caused these people great trouble and pain – rounding them up like animals to move them from place to place, telling them what they could and could not do, and even shooting them down in cold blood. The Paraguayans were Catholics. The Indians had seen them hold mass and believed that they were Christians. So they associated the word 'Christian' with those soldiers, and probably would kill anyone who claimed to be one. A beautiful word had been made repulsive and hateful through association.

"What word do I use instead?" I asked.

My interpreter answered, "Ask them to become a 'creyente,' a believer. After they are 'creyentes,' then you can explain that the word 'Christian' is not related to the army, or to guns and killing, but to life and love through Jesus Christ."

Think Before You Speak

Many times we would be wise to think carefully before we speak. A word may mean one thing to us but something entirely different to someone else. We also need to be careful how we use words to manipulate others. Parents are often guilty of using verbal threats and mis-information to control a child's behavior without giving proper thought to the indelible impressions they are making on young minds.

A friend of mine, Glen Johnson, is a missionary to Alaska. His work takes him to remote villages where white men are seldom seen. Arriving at one village with candy and little toys to hand out to the children, he was dismayed to see the little ones run screaming in terror to hide from him. Asking some Eskimo fathers why the children ran, he was told with a laugh, "It is because we tell them if they are bad we will give them to the white man, who will take them far away."

The fathers' thoughtless threats had created a deep fear in the children's hearts, making it impossible for them to receive Glen's offerings of friendship. That fear might well develop into a suspicion and hostility toward all foreigners in years to come. Parents should not instill unfounded fears to control a child's behavior.

(Lying tactics such as this are as effective on adults as

they are on children. Satan is a master of deceit. He plays on our imagination with fears of what might be and with fantasies of impending danger. Our own insecurities do the rest. Before we know it, we are behaving as if our fears are fact and the danger a reality.)

This same thoughtlessness can result in an insensitivity to other people's feelings, which can cause them to react with hostility. Shortly after I was married, a painful incident showed me how thoughtless and insensitive I could be.

Before my marriage, I traveled all over the world. During that time I heard lots of ethnic jokes. One night I attempted to amuse my in-laws by observing that throughout their history the British had proved themselves the bravest of soldiers. They had always fought to the last *Frenchman.*

It was an innocent little joke that would have been perfectly acceptable and inoffensive in the United States, but my wife's family are proud British Canadians. My father-in-law, a military man from way back, stood to his feet and exclaimed, "You can't say that kind of thing in my home!"

My thoughtless remark had offended rather than amused, and I learned the wisdom of forgetting jokes that buy laughter at the expense of someone else's dignity.

The Battle of the Mind

The human mind is a computer-like storage system of knowledge, past experiences, and learned responses. From the day we are born our "response systems" are being programmed. When a small child reaches out to touch the "pretty baby" reflected in the shiny side of a toaster, Mama yells, "Hot!" and he learns that "hot" means "Hurt. Don't touch."

The same is true of much more complicated emotional responses. When we have a painful or frightening experience, the next time a similar situation occurs we unconsciously prepare to be hurt or frightened again. Of course, much of this habitual response is healthy and works to our advantage as we learn from past mistakes. It is only when we become locked into behavior that is unloving or unproductive that we must stop and take stock.

We give in to impatience, anger, or resentment on one occasion and soon this becomes a way of life. The worst part is that often we accept these negative personality traits as part of our "natural makeup." "Oh, he just has a short fuse," we say of the man who can't seem to control his temper. Or we excuse someone's behavior by explaining, "She can't help being demanding; she's a perfectionist." Such people continue to be critical and impatient, and we really haven't done them a favor. It's much easier to blame emotional self-indulgence on "Mother Nature" than to recognize it as sin and submit it to the transforming discipline of the Holy Spirit.

Put off concerning the former conversation the old
man, which is corrupt according to the deceitful lusts;
And be renewed in the spirit of your mind;
And that ye put on the new man, which after God
is created in righteousness and true holiness.

Ephesians 4:22-24

The transformation from "old man" to "new man" is not automatic when we receive Christ. It is a result of our active obedience to the Scripture's admonition to "put off" or consciously reject the old lifestyle, to "be renewed" in our minds through prayer and the study of God's Word, and to "put on" the new image of Christlike behavior and attitudes. Again, the battle is in the mind; it has to do with the will.

The first step in accomplishing this radical change is to realize that none of us needs to be permanently enslaved to old emotional habits. Our minds are constantly making value judgments, deciding if something is good, bad, pleasant, or painful. We may have little control over our immediate emotional reaction to these things, but with the help of the Holy Spirit we can control our outward responses.

Both the world and the Bible agree that the "computer" can be reprogrammed. The world offers many different kinds of programs of self-analysis and mind control to achieve this end. Books have been written on the importance of controlling situations and not allowing situations to control us. We must learn to *act,* not *react.* One way to avoid hostile, negative confrontations, we are told by Theodora Wells in *Keeping Your Cool Under Fire,* is to learn to communicate nondefensively.

Learning to communicate nondefensively is easier said than done. It involves looking at some of your own attitudes, inner rules, and underlying beliefs that may contribute to feelings of defensiveness. In the process of becoming nondefensive you are also in the process of becoming more of your own person. . . . As you exercise more choices, you will be redefining yourself, renegotiating your relationships, and revising the results you get.[1]

It's not bad advice, as far as it goes. In essence, the writer is telling us to stop reacting with a preprogrammed response every time someone hits a certain emotional key. But even Wells admits that breaking that habit by sheer human determination is difficult at best.

---

[1]Theodora Wells, *Keeping Your Cool Under Fire* (New York: McGraw-Hill, 1980), p. 3.

Christians have a far more effective resource to draw from, found in Galatians 2:20:

> *I am crucified with Christ: nevertheless I live; yet not I, but Christ liveth in me: and the life which I now live in the flesh I live by the faith of the Son of God, who loved me, and gave himself for me.*

Christ living in me means I am no longer bound by old thought patterns or habitual responses. My life is no longer ruled by the old sin nature, but by God's love and mercy and His empowering Spirit.

The Apostle Paul had a wonderful, practical understanding of this truth. Helen Hosier explains this in her book, *It Feels Good To Forgive:*

> Paul knew what it meant to be mistreated by those who claimed to be brothers in Christ. But he submerged his hostility by saturating himself with thoughts of the forgiveness and love of Christ. It worked every time. Paul speaks from bitter experience. His word to us is that we too can have strength for all things in Christ Who empowers us....[2]

---

[2]Helen Hosier, *It Feels Good To Forgive* (Irvine, CA: Harvest House, 1979), p. 107.

15
Missing Ingredients in the Person Who Kills

Here are some of the key elements that are missing in the person who kills:

Friendship

Hostility has no roots of friendship. It has a way of destroying friendship, even among members of the same family.

A normal person would never kill a friend. He will do all kinds of good deeds for him and protect him, but he will never destroy him. Destruction comes from only one source: the devil.

God wants you to be a friend to others. He wants you to be friendly. He wants you to look at another person and say, "I'm your friend. I clasp your hand in friendship and love." A murderer cannot do that.

Pity

Hostility knows no pity. When we see a person who is hurting, we should have pity in our hearts for him and reach out to help.

How can a person brutally beat or stab a fellow human being and think of pity? That is not possible.

Pity heals. Pity reaches out and lifts up. Pity is being a good Samaritan, finding a stranger and taking him in, taking care of his needs.

Even in the jungle, oftentimes wild animals will adopt another animal not of its species or of its kind. They have even been known to find a lost child, adopt it, give it suck, and provide for it.

A person who commits murder is certainly not trying to heal the hurts of another person or family. There was no pity in Stephen Judy. (See chapter 2.) He raped and brutally murdered a young mother, then destroyed the lives of her three small children. These were people he had never seen before. The murders were totally unprovoked.

Forgiveness

There is no forgiveness in hostility and in murder. Many times, murder resulted because one person could not forgive another person. The opposite of this can be seen clearly in the ministry of our Lord Jesus Christ.

Jesus had a spirit of forgiveness. He even forgave Judas Iscariot, the man who had betrayed Him.

As the Romans were nailing Him to the cross and the Jews were laughing and mocking Him, Jesus said with love, "Father, forgive them. They don't know what they are doing. They don't understand. Forgive them, Father."

The spirit of forgiveness is a heavenly spirit. The spirit of anger and hostility is demonic and will culminate in murder.

Compassion

One of the greatest descriptions in the life of the Lord Jesus was that He had compassion. He had compassion on the multitudes.

Hostility has no compassion. Hate has no compassion. These satanic forces are killers, destroyers; but the Spirit of Jesus is compassion.

When the Master said, "I will have compassion on the multitude," it moved Him to act. He lifted their hunger and their sickness from them. He lifted their pain and their sorrow from them. Why? Because He had compassion.

Compassion is the divine ability to enter into another person's sorrow and help him. Unprovoked murder is the very opposite of that. It kills. It brings sorrow. It creates problems. Acts of unprovoked murder are not human, and they certainly are not divine.

Study any of the cases of unprovoked murder and you will see people who are without compassion. Even after they were sentenced to death, they had no feeling.

After killing eight nurses in Chicago, Richard Speck was asked, "Do you have any remorse?"

He answered simply, "No. They're dead."

After killing the young mother and her three little children, Stephen Judy was asked, "Any remorse?"

"No. That's past."

That shows you just how far removed God is from such situations.

Rather than help the person, they hurt them. Rather than have feelings of compassion toward the person, they desired to destroy them.

Hostility Must Be Stopped

Hostility breeds like an epidemic of cholera. It won't stop by itself. It must be stopped! You must not let hostility grow, especially in the lives of children. You must stop it!

It is obvious that hostility is a symptom which produces unprovoked murder.

According to First John 4:20, you cannot love God and hate a brother. If you claim to be a Christian and say you love God, you cannot hate your brother. If you hate a brother, the love of God is not in you.

Jesus said in John 8:44 that the devil was a murderer from the beginning. All taking of life comes from him.

16
Facing Up to Hostility

You've heard it said that recognizing a problem is half the battle. So it is with hostility. Most of us have no difficulty seeing hostility in others, but identifying it in our own lives is another matter. It is very easy for us to justify our feelings or to label them as something they are not.

If you detect suppressed hostility in someone and, out of love and concern, you ask them, "Why are you hostile?" more than likely you will get an emphatic denial. Moreover, the person questioned will no doubt react with hostility. Furthermore, they will be quick to try to convince you that they are anything but hostile. "I'm not hostile, but I am hurt," they might say, or "I've been left out and ignored, and I'm really disappointed."

We must stop making excuses and face up to the problem of hostility – not just in other people but within our own hearts and minds – if we are ever to make a significant difference in the world around us. We may not be able to stop the acceleration of hostility throughout the earth, but we can protect our own private world of thoughts and attitudes and personal relationships from its ravaging effects.

Civilized man has proved that he is capable of behaving in a most uncivilized way. Lifting a man's mind out of the Dark Ages has nothing to do with lifting his soul out of spiritual darkness. Hostility is a fact of life on planet earth; it will exist until Jesus comes. Evil and iniquity will be with us until the prince of this world is cast down. For this reason we must learn to cope with sin and hostility in a godly way.

Pray, Talk, and Then Do Something!

Some might say, "Brother Sumrall, you are writing about a spiritual problem, so let's not talk about it; let's pray about it."

I say, "Let's do both." Prayer is an essential weapon in the battle, and I am by no means disparaging its power and effect. But the Word says that faith without works is dead, and I believe that American Christians have been silent for too long. A recent nationwide poll revealed that 58 percent of all Americans profess to be born again! It is time we spoke up for righteousness with a loud voice. We *can* make a difference.

But people won't hear us if we refuse to be honest about our own failures and weaknesses. We must take the positive steps necessary to live lives that manifest the power and love of God in practical, everyday situations. One of those steps is facing up to and dealing with our own hostility.

One's ability to deal with anger, hatred, prejudice, jealousy, and other hostile emotions depends on his spiritual understanding and his conscious desire to overcome the problems. Only when we recognize them, admit they are our own, and submit them to God's transforming power can we be truly free. Unfortunately, some people have buried their hostility so deep that they are totally unaware that it is there. There are people who make it a practice never to argue, thereby claiming they have learned to control their tempers. The truth is, their hostility is being suppressed. Avoiding arguments and maintaining a calm exterior all the time is not realistic.

We come back to Ephesians 4:26. *Be ye angry, and sin not: let not the sun go down upon your wrath.* God does not tell us that in order to be holy we must put on some false, sanctimonious show; rather, He encourages us to express our indignation over things that are wrong. By this means we keep our emotional system cleaned out; the anger has no opportunity to dam up inside and cause problems.

The Dangers of Passive Hostility

It is a fact of life that there is no such thing as a person who never gets angry. There are only those who express their anger, and those who suppress it. According to Alan Loy McGinnis, people who don't express their anger in a healthy way not only develop psychological problems but also put their important personal relationships in jeopardy. The mild-mannered man may appear to be more popular, but according to McGinnis, popularity is not synonymous with intimacy. The man who is super-ficially liked by everyone is rarely loved deeply by anyone.

McGinnis lists four reasons he believes this is true of the passively hostile person.

1. He is never perceived as open, so he is hard for others to relate to.
2. He is dull. People prefer the company of others with more passion.
3. If he cannot show anger he will be inept at showing love as well.
4. Without knowing it, he poisons his relationships with his passive hostility.[1]

It is a recognized fact that passively hostile people are much harder to get along with than those who erupt with

[1]Alan Loy McGinnis. *The Friendship Factor* (Minneapolis, MN: Augsburg, 1979), p. 128.

honest, direct anger. Passively hostile people show by their actions that they have been hurt, but they deny that anything is wrong. The result of living this way is that the acids of accumulating grudges eat away at their relationships.

Elizabeth Skoglund, who wrote *To Anger, With Love*, believes anger is unavoidable when two people relate openly and spontaneously, and that it can be a positive force when expressed in a healthy way.

I have heard this inevitable "abrasiveness" in relationships described as a "sandpaper effect." One of the major purposes for God's bringing two people together, whether in marriage or as friends, is so that each may encourage the other. That encouragement can be pleasant or not, depending on how receptive we are to what we are being told. Much of our "remodeling" requires a sanding away of rough surfaces and sharp edges – not particularly comfortable but necessary.

When we recognize this constant rubbing not as an irritant, but as the loving hand of our heavenly Father polishing us to a high shine in which others will see the reflection of Christ, it becomes easier to accept without giving way to hostility.

Overt Hostility

For the overtly hostile person, the first step in facing up to hostility is admitting his attitude is wrong. This presents a challenge. Hostility usually is triggered by someone else's negative or thoughtless action toward us, so it is easy to excuse or rationalize our hostile response.

When our hostility has grounds for defense, we often choose to nurture our feelings, feeding our anger instead of releasing it and trusting the Lord to rectify the situation.

A pair of newlyweds have their first no-holds-barred argument, and it ends with the bride making a dramatic retreat to the bedroom and locking the door. For the next half hour, her distraught young husband listens to her loud sobs. Finally, unable to stand it any longer, he knocks on the door.

"Please, Honey, open the door. I want to apologize."

"Later," she answers. "I'm not through being mad yet!"

Something inside the human heart *enjoys* being angry when we feel we've been wronged. We don't want to let go of it; we savor our indignation and reaffirm our position as a "victim."

Some people become so steeped in what they regard as "justified anger" that it becomes the strongest part of their personalities, tainting every other area of thought and expression. Their anger protects them from feelings of vulnerability and helplessness, and so becomes a strange ally in their battle against despair. Soon, their hostility becomes a motivation rather than a result, a living thing that no longer can be traced to any one hurt, but actually propagates itself.

At this point a person's whole identity can become directly linked to his anger, which becomes very difficult to isolate and identify. When this happens, human logic no longer has any effect. Only the Word of God, which is sharper than any two-edged sword, can cut through to the root and cull it out.

For this reason Psalm 37:7-9 urges:

Rest in the Lord, and wait patiently for him: fret not thyself because of him who prospereth in his way, because of the man who bringeth wicked devices to pass.

Cease from anger, and forsake wrath: fret not thyself in any wise to do evil.

For evildoers shall be cut off: but those that wait upon the Lord, they shall inherit the earth.

No matter what injustice we may have suffered or how unkind someone may have been, we are responsible for our own actions and attitudes. We have available to us all the resources necessary to have victory over sinful or negative feelings through Christ our Lord. Once we face up to this responsibility, we are ready to take action to destroy hostility in our lives.

17
How To Destroy Hostility

One cannot improve upon God's method for dealing with hostility. In Galatians 5:16-25 we are given the directions for living a love-inspired, love-mastered, and love-driven life.

Walking in the Spirit

This I say then, Walk in the Spirit, and ye shall not fulfil the lust of the flesh.

For the flesh lusteth against the Spirit, and the Spirit against the flesh: and these are contrary the one to the other: so that ye cannot do the things that ye would.

But if ye be led of the Spirit, ye are not under the law.

Now the works of the flesh are manifest, which are these; adultery, fornication, uncleanness, lasciviousness,

Idolatry, witchcraft, hatred, variance, emulations, wrath, strife, seditions, heresies,

Envyings, murders, drunkenness, revellings, and such like: of the which I tell you before, as I have also told you in time past, that they which do such things shall not inherit the kingdom of God.

But the fruit of the Spirit is love, joy, peace, longsuffering, gentleness, goodness, faith,

Meekness, temperance: against such there is no law.

And they that are Christ's have crucified the flesh with the affections and lusts.

If we live in the Spirit, let us also walk in the Spirit.

Every one of the "works of the flesh" is related to hostility in some way. It is the fruit of the Spirit that counterbalances their negative effects. But while the works of the flesh spring up like weeds in an unattended garden, the fruit of the Spirit must be carefully cultivated. This can be done only through a personal relationship with Jesus Christ, through reading His Word, and through making a conscious effort to pull out the "weeds" as they creep back into our thoughts and actions.

The Power of Confession

Once we face up to hostility, we need to verbally confess it to the Lord. The power of confession cleanses the soul, keeping us open to God's continuous work of redemption in our lives. As we seek to be more like Jesus, we will find the fruit of the Spirit more evident in us. At the same time, our human nature, which leads to hostility, will be more easily subjugated.

For a good tree bringeth not forth corrupt fruit; neither doth a corrupt tree bring forth good fruit.

For every tree is known by his own fruit. For of thorns men do not gather figs, nor of a bramble bush gather they grapes.

A good man out of the good treasure of his heart bringeth forth that which is good; and an evil man out of the evil treasure of his heart bringeth forth that which is evil: for of the abundance of the heart his mouth speaketh.

Luke 6:43-45

You Are Being Heard

If you want to know who you really are, just listen to what you say. The mouth speaks what is in the heart. If our hearts are bound with cords of bitterness and grudges, we may say the right words but we will communicate our hostility loud and clear by our tone and inflection. But as we humble ourselves and allow the Holy Spirit to transform our hearts and renew our minds, our attitudes and conversation will be a direct reflection of the love of Jesus working in us and through us.

It is only by the mighty power of God that hostility is defeated and driven from our hearts. But certain principles from God's Word provide us with the major weapons for this battle.

Forgiveness

Forgiveness is perhaps the most powerful and essential of these weapons; without it there can be no release from hostility. Forgiveness is an act of the will. It has nothing to do with the rightness or wrongness of our grievance or whether the other person is repentant or not. We must forgive as we have been forgiven.

Many people pray these familiar words: *And forgive us our debts, as we forgive our debtors* (Matthew 6:12). But I wonder how many of us actually think about what we are asking when we say those words.

Jesus said, *If ye forgive not men their trespasses, neither will your Father forgive your trespasses* (Matthew 6:15).

Clearly, if we do not forgive, we shall not be forgiven.

C. S. Lewis, in his book *Mere Christianity,* discussed two things that can help make forgiveness something we do, not just something we talk about doing:

1. Start with smaller hurts, which are more easily forgiven, and work up to the truly heart-crushing injustices life brings.
2. Come to a clearer understanding of what it means to "love thy neighbor as thyself."

    . . . I have not exactly got a feeling of fondness

or affection for myself, and I do not even always enjoy my own society. So apparently "love your neighbor" does not mean "feel fond of him" or "find him attractive." I ought to have seen that before, because, of course, you cannot feel fond of a person by trying. . . .

. . . a good many people imagine that forgiving your enemies means making out that they are really not such bad fellows after all, when it is quite plain that they are. Go a step further. In my most clear-sighted moments not only do I not think myself a nice man, but I know that I am a very nasty one. I can look at some of the things I have done with horror and loathing. So apparently I am allowed to loathe and hate some of the things my enemies do. Now that I come to think of it, I remember Christian teachers telling me long ago that I must hate a bad man's actions, but not hate the bad man: or, as they would say, hate the sin but not the sinner.

For a long time I used to think this a silly, straw-splitting distinction: how could you hate what a man did and not hate the man? But years later it occurred to me that there was one man to whom I had been doing this all my life – namely myself. However much I might dislike my own cowardice or conceit or greed, I went on loving myself. There had never been the slightest difficulty about it. In fact, the very reason why I hated the things was that I loved the man. Just because I loved myself, I was sorry to find that I was the sort of man who did those things. Consequently, Christianity does not want us to reduce by one atom the hatred we feel for cruelty and treachery. We ought to hate them. Not one word of what we have said about them needs to be unsaid. But it does want us to hate them in the same way in which we hate things in ourselves: being sorry that the man should have done such things, and hoping, if it is any way possible, that somehow, sometime, somewhere, he can be cured and made human again.[1]

Honest Confrontation

This willingness to forgive others does not obligate us to swallow our feelings when we honestly believe a brother has wronged us. This kind of suppression can lead to the unhealthy emotional buildup that produces the very hostility we are determined to destroy. Matthew 18:15 tells us how to handle these situations:

Moreover if thy brother shall trespass against thee, go and tell him his fault between thee and him alone: if he shall hear thee, thou hast gained thy brother.

Honest confrontation aimed toward reconciliation will safeguard us from a buildup of negative emotions and help to keep lines of communication open. If we can talk about our feelings honestly, we have a much better chance of keeping them under control and of resolving the issue without damaging the relationship or our own spiritual and emotional health.

Prayer

Prayer is a mighty weapon against hostility. If we truly believe that *whatsoever thou shalt bind on earth shall be bound in heaven: and whatsoever thou shalt loose on earth shall be loosed in heaven* (Matthew 16:19), then we know we are never helpless in any situation. We have all the resources

---

[1]C. S. Lewis, *Mere Christianity* (New York: Macmillan, 1943), pp. 105,106.

of heaven at our disposal. This knowledge in itself should help check the hostility-producing fears and frustrations that come with a seemingly hopeless situation. Christians are never hopeless or helpless, because they serve a God Who can do anything and Who answers prayer.

There are times when bondage to hostility is so deep-seated that deliverance is needed. If this is the case, don't be afraid. Talk to your pastor or a discerning Christian counselor. Jesus came to heal the brokenhearted and deliver the captives. The bonds of hostility are strong, and you may need the prayers of other believers to break their hold.

Accept and Appreciate Others

Accepting other people and circumstances is another practical step in destroying hostility. Don't torture yourself with what might have been. Don't allow Satan to needle you into dissatisfaction with your lot in life. Trust God, knowing that He gives each of His children exactly what he or she needs.

Get in the habit of appreciating other people's good qualities. Will Rogers was famous for his saying, "I never met a man I didn't like." He approached others expecting the best, and people usually made an effort not to disappoint him. Much of our attitude toward other people is determined long before we even meet them. A positive acceptance of others does much to dispel hostility.

Resist feelings of competitiveness, which can make you resent another's success. Instead, rejoice in your brother's good fortune and do your best to follow Paul's admonition: *Let nothing be done through strife or vainglory; but in lowliness of mind let each esteem other better than themselves* (Philippians 2:3).

If you make the people around you feel good about themselves, you will reap the benefit of their confidence and positive attitude, and hostility will be far less likely to find a foothold.

When conflicts do arise, take time to put yourself in the other person's position. Sometimes this provides an entirely different picture of the situation. If you cannot acquiesce, perhaps you can at least compromise with good humor and grace.

We can avoid overreacting to negative situations if we realize that disagreements are bound to happen in any relationship. Don't have unrealistic expectations of yourself or of others. Recognize that frustration and anger are emotions we all feel at times; the best relationships allow for such things.

Parent-Child Relationships

These principles also apply to parent-child relationships. Children are people, too, and they need to express their negative feelings just as adults do. If little Johnny is punished every time he expresses anger or frustration, he will grow up habitually suppressing his negative emotions. With no understanding of how to release those emotions in a healthy way, he becomes a walking time bomb. Parents must teach children appropriate ways to communicate these feelings, without being overly permissive or encouraging emotional self-indulgence.

In this regard it is helpful for parents to understand that anger and sadness are closely related in childhood. A small child has not as yet developed a working understanding of all the varied shades of negative and positive emotions. Instead he lumps them together under far more basic headings such as happy, sad, glad, and mad. Once this is understood it becomes obvious that some expression of anger or frustration is completely normal and to some degree necessary for healthy emotional development.

The following are a few practical suggestions for dealing with the angry or hostile child:

1. Respond to positive efforts and reinforce good behavior. We are quick to tell a child what we don't like. Be equally quick to tell him what we do like.
2. Avoid placing a small child in a situation that you know will provoke or tempt him beyond his emotional ability to control.
3. Teach a child to see humor in even difficult situations. The healthiest people are the ones who have learned to laugh at themselves once in a while.
4. Talk to your child about your feelings regarding his behavior. Don't always just say "no." Explain possible consequences so that the child understands your reasoning. This is what the Bible means by *train up a child in the way he should go* . . . taking the time to instruct as well as to correct.
5. Create clearly defined and easily understood limits.
6. Encourage the child to talk about his feelings and really listen when he does. If a child learns early to verbalize his feelings, he will find it less necessary later to resort to violent or destructive behavior.
7. Show your affection and constantly remind the child that he is loved and wanted.

Teaching a child to deal with his emotions is a most pressing and demanding responsibility for parents because children learn best from examples, not lectures. "Do as I say and not as I do" simply doesn't work. Essential to helping a child handle his anger is the ability on the part of the parent to do the same with his or her feelings of hostility. Angry parents who cannot control their own anger will be unable to help children who have feelings of hostility.

Walter Trobisch tells of observing hostility directed toward children in his travels from country to country. I, too, have observed this. He believes we in the "so-called Christian West" are more guilty of this than parents in Third World countries and some of the Iron Curtain countries.

Trobisch relates this to the abortion problem in this country:

> It seems to me that there is a direct relationship between the lack of self-acceptance, the hostility toward the body and the hostility toward children. Bringing forth children is a part of the physical dimension of life. He who does not have a positive relationship to his body will find it difficult to reach a positive relationship to the child, who is a fruit of his body.
>
> I wonder whether one of the deepest roots of the abortion problem does not lie here. Could it be that this also is the result of non-self-acceptance which expresses itself in a hostile act against the newborn fruit of the body? Can an expectant mother who wishes to abort her child really love herself? Otherwise how could she act so egotistically?[2]

Hostility is much easier to avoid if we discipline ourselves to deal with the issues as they arise. Don't let a dozen small irritations that could easily be talked out one at a time create a wall of cumulative bad feelings between you and someone else. And be sure your anger is focused upon the real issue, not on someone or something else. For many of us this will take thought and discipline,

---

[2]Walter Trobisch, *Love Yourself* (Downers Grove, IL: InterVarsity, 1976), pp. 32,33.

because it is easy to fall into the habit of using those we feel secure with as emotional "whipping boys."

Parents especially must be careful not to abuse their children by taking advantage of minor offenses to blow off steam, just as anyone in a position of authority must guard himself from abusing his power. It is sad but quite generally true that authority figures tend to be quick to anger. When such individuals can't find an appropriate outlet, they often vent their anger towards someone who can't easily fight back – an employee, a child, a spouse, or an animal.

David Augsburger suggests that another practical way to control hostility is to zero in on the specific behavior we don't like rather than attacking the whole person.

> Next time, try focusing your anger on the person's behavior. Express appreciation for the other as a person, even as you explain your anger at his or her way of behaving. It lets you stay in touch while getting at what you are angry about. And, as Jesus demonstrated, you can be both angry (at behaviors) and loving (toward persons) at the same time.[3]

Refuse to play the "blame game." Since we are all ultimately responsible before God for our own behavior and attitudes, it is a waste of time and energy to attempt to place blame or inflict guilt upon others.

> Blame is powerless to effect change and growth. Blame is powerless to evoke inner-direction and new course correction. . . . Nothing settles old scores like the recognition that everything finally comes out even. That's how it

---

[3]David Augsburger, *Caring Enough To Confront* (Glendale, CA: Regal, 1973), p. 41.

is in any ongoing relationship. If there is blame to be fixed, it includes both persons involved.[4]

Think Before You Speak

Learn to express your feelings clearly. Heated arguments are generally ineffective because it is impossible to think rationally, to speak thoughtfully, and to really hear what the other person is saying when you are in the throes of emotional combat. Instead, take a few moments to think through what you want to say. Count to ten.

By controlling our tongues and reining in our unbridled emotions, we can actually turn negative confrontations into creative and positive exchanges that have the power to break through emotional and communication barriers and establish contact.

Once channels of communication are open, hostility usually gives way to a mutual desire to understand and solve the problem. When this happens, the relationship is strengthened, not weakened. Most of us know how it feels to air grievances and then get the relationship back on the right track.

Anger's Energy: A Positive Force

We needn't always look at anger as an enemy. There are certain things we should be angry about. There are times when God uses anger over evil or injustice in the world to spur men into action against it. Powerful indignation has fired the careers of many influential men. Martin Luther once said, "When I am angry I can write, pray, and preach well, for my whole temperament is quickened, my understanding sharpened, and all mundane vexations and temptations depart."

---

[4]*Ibid., pp. 76,77.*

Anger quickens the senses, shooting adrenaline through our bodies and glycogen to our fatigued muscles. It moves the lethargic to action, giving courage for tasks we would never attempt in milder moods.

Anger need not rule our lives; rather, we can rule over it, using it as a positive instrument to produce change and growth. The energy anger produces can be a powerful force when controlled by love and an awareness of the other person's rights and worth.

In *The Friendship Factor*, Alan Loy McGinnis suggests five ways to get angry without being destructive:

1. *"Talk about your feelings, not your friend's faults. . . .* To express our irritation in terms of our feelings, for which we are willing to take responsibility, does not insure protection from our friend's anger, but it is a lot less likely to wave a red flag."[5]

2. *"Stick to one topic. . . .* The resolution of one problem at a time is difficult enough without pulling in old grievances. The problems should be dealt with as they arise, so that we do not carry around unprocessed anger."[6]

3. *"Allow your friend to respond. . . .* People who walk out during an argument are dirty fighters. If you are angry with your friend, you have a right to express it, but you also have the responsibility to stay and hear the other side. Then there's an opportunity for resolution or compromise."[7]

4. *"Aim for ventilation, not conquest. . . .* The point of showing our loved ones our anger is to ventilate our feelings, not to force them to surrender. Far

---

[5]Alan Loy McGinnis, *The Friendship Factor* (Minneapolis, MN: Augsburg, 1979), p. 140.
[6]Ibid., p. 142.
[7]Ibid.

too many couples suppose that every time there is an argument, one or the other has to apologize. Apologies are sometimes in order and sometimes they are not. Lots of times it clears the air if the two ventilate their emotions, get their hostility out, and then go back to loving each other. No one has to win."[8]

5. *"Balance criticism with lots of affection. . . .* You can get away with many expressions of anger if you balance them with lots of expressions of love."[9]

The last point is very important. Rarely do we forget to tell someone when we are angered, hurt, or irritated by something they have said or done. But frequently we don't think to speak aloud our admiration or appreciation for family members, close friends, or fellow workers. We take the good things for granted, while never missing a chance to point out the bad. People try harder to please when their efforts are acknowledged, and they receive criticism and correction more easily from someone who has already demonstrated his respect and appreciation for them as individuals.

"Walking Love"

Unquestionably, our lives will be stronger, richer, and have more meaning in direct proportion to our willingness to express love. We are to be "walking love" to each other.

Love! Love is the key: God's love for us, our love for ourselves, and our love for others. Hostility may be contagious, but so is love. And where love abounds, hostility cannot thrive. In his book, *A Second Touch*, Keith

---

[8]Ibid., p. 143.
[9]Ibid., p. 144.

Miller talks about how his revitalized awareness of God's love and concern for him personally helped him to begin seeing and responding to others in a whole new way.

Being conscious of Christ's attention not only affected what I did and said, but what I saw. And just seeing people differently changed entire relationships. There was one man, whom I disliked intensely, whose office was close to ours. He was arrogant and a smart aleck; he needled people viciously, many of whom, like the secretaries, could only choke back tears of embarrassment and anger. This man was mad at the world. As an angry smart aleck (which is what I saw when I looked at him), he had no use for Christ's love. But as I began to look at this man, being aware that Christ and I were looking at him together, I began to see in the same person a man who was deeply hurt, threatened, and very lonely. This is what this man really was inside. It dawned on me that for a man like that, Christ's love could have meaning. When I responded naturally to what I now saw as I looked at this man, he began to drop the facade of anger, and hurt began to come out. Suddenly we were at ease with each other without anything having been said to break down the real person behind his mask, and somehow he knew and felt loved. I was seeing why the saints had come up with such seemingly simple, basic ways to relate. It was not because they were brilliant. Most of them were not. They had a different perspective; and from that spiritual vantage point, they looked at the unsolvable problems other men saw. However, they saw – in the same situations – different problems. They saw problems which

could be dealt with through the love and acceptance of God. They saw men as Christ saw them.[10]

Once we begin to see other people as Jesus sees them,
with all their hurts, insecurities, and loneliness, we find it
possible to love our neighbors and our enemies. We can
love those who don't love us or even like us. When they
make a little circle and leave us out, we can make a bigger
circle and take them in. And there isn't anything they can
do about it; they are loved.

Love frees us to allow other people to be what God
intended them to be, not what we think they should be.
And it helps us to accept our own flaws and frailties. The
God Who created us accepts our humanity, including our
hostile feelings. What He wants is our willingness to yield
to His Holy Spirit, so He can turn all our emotions in the
right direction.

God can use our anger in positive ways, but it is not
enough to give Him only our anger. We must give Him
our hearts, our thoughts, our ambitions for the future, and
our hurts of the past. We must relinquish our rights to
bitterness and resentment, just as Jesus did even as they
drove the nails into His hands and feet. We must seek to
be filled with an understanding of His will.

That ye might walk worthy of the Lord unto all
pleasing, being fruitful in every good work, and
increasing in the knowledge of God;

Strengthened with all might, according to his
glorious power, unto all patience and longsuffering with
joyfulness;

Giving thanks unto the Father, which hath made
us meet to be partakers of the inheritance of the saints
in light:

---

[10]Keith Miller, *A Second Touch* (Waco, TX: Word, 1967), pp, 28,29.

*Who hath delivered us from the power of darkness,
and hath translated us into the kingdom of his dear Son:
In whom we have redemption through his blood,
even the forgiveness of sins.*

Colossians 1:10-14

Jesus' death and resurrection provide a way for us to be free from hostility and from all other sinful bondage. We who are His children are no longer bound to the "works of the flesh." We can resign ourselves to lives of slavery, to old thought patterns and emotional responses, or we can assume the responsibilities of our liberty in Christ Jesus, with all its privileges and demands.

The bondage of hostility or the freedom of love, the choice is ours.

If the Son therefore shall make you free, ye shall be free indeed.

John 8:36

18

What Jesus Said and Did About Hostility

Then came Peter to him, and said, Lord, how oft shall my brother sin against me, and I forgive him? till seven times?

Jesus saith unto him, I say not unto thee, Until seven times: but, Until seventy times seven.

Matthew 18:21,22

This Scripture passage expresses the Master's heart about hostility. Forgive, not seven times but seventy times seven. There is to be no limit to our forgiveness. Jesus knew that forgiveness destroys hostility. Where there is a willingness to forgive, there is no place for anger, hurt feelings, or bitterness and resentment to take root.

Jesus' Instructions

In the Sermon on the Mount, Jesus gave very specific instructions about how to avoid hostility:

But I say unto you, That ye resist not evil: but whosoever shall smite thee on thy right cheek, turn to him the other also.

Matthew 5:39

This Scripture verse deals with our willingness to remain vulnerable and open. The physical action of being struck in the face can be symbolic of any hurt or wrong we experience at the hands of another. Jesus was not concerned with the injustice of the act, but with the attitude and response of the one who has been wronged.

Through faith and the power of the Holy Spirit, Who enables us to do any and all good things, we can learn not to spontaneously *react* in anger, but to retain control of the situation by *choosing* to forgive. It will be possible to "turn the other cheek" instead of hitting back. By this *action* we turn a negative situation into an expression of love and forgiveness, which probably will disarm the other person and very possibly open the door for real reconciliation. At the very least we will be strengthened in our own resolve not to be manipulated by someone else's anger and sin.

Jesus went on to say, *And if any man will sue thee at the law, and take away thy coat, let him have thy cloak also* (Matthew 5:40).

Again Jesus was addressing the attitude of the one being wronged. Life can be unfair. The innocent aren't always vindicated. The best man doesn't always win. Maybe you have worked hard at a job for ten years and your boss promotes someone else who's only been there five years. Or, as in the example Jesus used, perhaps you were taken to court and lost a case you should have won. What is your response going to be? Bitterness? Anger? Resentment? If you allow these things to fester inside, you will lose more than your coat. You will forfeit peace of mind, the joy of life, and the confidence of a right standing before God. That kind of hostility is costly and fruitless.

Instead, Jesus said, give up your rights and privileges. Refuse to fantasize about what might have been or argue about what should have been. Ask the Holy Spirit to help you keep things in the right perspective. The loss of a coat isn't all that tragic. In fact, the loss of a coat *and* a cloak isn't going to destroy your life. But bitterness and resentment will. Jesus was saying that a key to defeating hostility is to recognize what our true treasures and privileges really are.

And whosoever shall compel thee to go a mile, go with him twain (Matthew 5:41). I've heard it said that a Roman citizen had the authority to compel any slave to carry his things as far as a mile. This may have been what Jesus was referring to. When someone begins throwing his weight around and making unreasonable demands, it is human nature to dig our heels in and resist. No one likes to be taken advantage of or used for another's selfish purposes. Although for the most part we are no longer legally bound to "walk that mile" with another person, we are constantly facing the demands of family, friends, and employers. The question is, how much are we willing to give joyfully, and how many of those demands are we going to meet with the right attitude?

Jesus said if a man compels you to go a mile, surprise him and go two. By this means you take control of the situation. You are no longer being taken advantage of; rather, you are accepting an opportunity to give, and you will be blessed for it. Since you are doing something of your own free will, resentment has no room to grow.

In all three examples, Jesus was dealing with the heart attitude of the one wronged. In every case, that person would have had "just cause" to be angry, bitter, or resentful.

Obviously, He knew it would not be easy for us to give and forgive as He directed. Nowhere did He suggest we are going to be supernaturally lifted above our natural, human reactions to these difficult situations. But we know that God does not require anything from us that He also doesn't enable us to perform. Clearly, the message is that no matter how extreme or unjust the situation may be, we sons and daughters of God are not to become hostile.

Corrie ten Boom is a living example of one who determined to forgive and who refused to be hostile. In her book, *Tramp for the Lord,* Corrie recounts a particularly poignant and difficult confrontation she had with her own struggle to forgive. In a church in Munich she met one of the men who had been a guard at Ravensbruck, the Nazi concentration camp in which she was imprisoned and where her sister Betsie died.

It was 1947, and she had come from Holland to defeated Germany with the message that God forgives. As the man thrust out his hand to her he said, "A fine message, Fraulein! How good it is to know that, as you say, all our sins are at the bottom of the sea!"

Corrie, who moments before had spoken so glibly of forgiveness, now found herself fumbling in her pocketbook rather than taking the man's hand. She remembered only too well the leather crop swinging from his belt and the cruelties the prisoners had endured.

The man explained that he had been a guard at Ravensbruck, but that since that time he had become a Christian. He knew God had forgiven him for the cruel things he had done there, he said, but he wanted to know if Corrie, too, would forgive him. Again he reached out his hand.

Seconds seemed like hours as Corrie wrestled inwardly. Could the memory of Betsie's slow, terrible death be cleared away with a handshake? Yet Corrie knew God had forgiven her own sins again and again – could she do any less for someone who had wronged her and now sought her forgiveness?

She prayed that Jesus would help her.

Numbly she raised her hand to his, and as they

grasped she felt a healing warmth through her whole being. "I forgive you, brother, with all my heart!" she cried.

But even as she spoke she knew it was not her love; she had been powerless to love on her own. She could only love by the power of the Holy Spirit.

Jesus gave us a classic and beautiful example of forgiveness in the story of the prodigal son. An ungrateful son rebelled against his parents, demanded his inheritance, and left home, only to lose everything and come back repentant and willing to be a servant in his father's house. Instead, his father welcomed him home with open arms and ordered a great feast to celebrate his return.

But his brother was angry and resentful and refused to enter into the festivities. When his father asked why, he replied, "Because I've been the good son, doing everything you wanted, and you've never given me a party like this."

The brother was jealous and filled with pious indignation over what he regarded as unfair treatment. His hurt pride made it impossible for him to enter into the family's joy or to empathize with his brother's situation. It seems that in his eyes his brother's greatest sin was repenting and coming home again.

This brother's hostility should be a reminder to all of us to guard against any judgmental spirit that might keep us from wholeheartedly welcoming back into our church or circle of acquaintances those who wander away, fall into sin, and then return broken and needing our love and understanding to become whole again.

The Spiritual Consequences of Hostility

Jesus dealt with the spiritual consequences of hostility. He said:

*Ye have heard that it was said by them of old time,
Thou shalt not kill; and whosoever shall kill shall be in
danger of the judgment:*

*But I say unto you, That whosoever is angry with
his brother without a cause shall be in danger of the
judgment: and whosoever shall say to his brother, Raca,
shall be in danger of the council: but whosoever shall
say, Thou fool, shall be in danger of hell fire.*

Matthew 5:21,22

Most of us have no conception of the spiritual dynamic
of feelings such as anger and hate when directed toward
another person. When released in a healthy way, that
dynamic can be positive, breathing new life into relationships and personalities. But when allowed to ferment into
hostility, it can be deathly, slowly squeezing the life out of
vital areas of the soul.

At the same time, Jesus warned that harboring hostile
feelings places us in danger of "judgment" and "hell fire."

An Example To Follow

By far, the most profound commentary we have on
hostility is not what Jesus said about it, but how He
dealt with it personally. From the moment He was born,
Jesus was confronted with others' hatred, fear, and resentment. Barely hours old, He was forced to flee the mass
slaughter of newborns that King Herod had ordered in
hopes of catching Jesus among them.

Jesus' early years were quiet enough. *And Jesus
increased in wisdom and stature, and in favour with God and
man* (Luke 2:52). As long as He conformed to the accepted
way of thinking and living, He was liked and encouraged.
But the moment He stepped outside that familiar pattern
and began proclaiming His message and manifesting His
authority, His existence became a threat, challenging the

traditional foundations of man's relationship to God and man's relationship to man. Those who could not accept the truth and the transformation of thought and life it demanded became hostile and fearful, desiring only to silence His voice.

Matthew, chapter 8, tells about a demon-possessed man who lived among some tombs in the country of the Gergesenes. The man was violent and would attack anyone who passed that way. Jesus freed that man from his torment by casting the devils into a herd of pigs, which promptly ran down a steep hill into the sea and drowned.

> *And they that kept them fled, and went their ways into the city, and told every thing, and what was befallen to the possessed of the devils.*
>
> *And, behold, the whole city came out to meet Jesus: and when they saw him, they besought him that he would depart out of their coasts.*
>
> *And he entered into a ship, and passed over, and came into his own city.*
>
> Matthew 8:33-9:1

The people didn't understand what had happened. They were angry at the loss of the pigs and frightened by the inexplicable events. Their anger and fear produced hostility that closed their minds and their eyes to a miracle. No one was the least bit concerned about the man who had been delivered. Somehow his miraculous transformation was overshadowed by the loss of the pigs.

Yet Jesus didn't argue the point with the people. He didn't stand the delivered man up in front of them and say, "Look what I did!" He didn't call them a bunch of selfish ingrates and swear never to come back again. He simply got in a boat and left quietly. When we don't want Jesus around, He doesn't get angry. He just goes away. But He never harbors a grudge.

Jesus came back to these people at a later date. In the meantime, the people had calmed down and become conscious of the man who had been freed from the devils. He had told everyone what God had done for him, and when Jesus returned the people were ready to listen.

Jesus knew how to be patient with people's fears and insecurities. Since He knew their hearts, He was tolerant of those who were motivated by an honest desire to know God, even if occasionally they were a little hard of hearing or stubborn. But when they were motivated by greed or selfish ambition, He was capable of the righteous anger and indignation He demonstrated against the money changers in the temple. This incident in Jesus' life substantiates the premise that anger in itself is not always a sin nor a negative force. While there is no room in our lives for bitter hostility, at times anger is appropriate.

Certainly anger is a difficult emotion to control. Not only does it arouse our adrenaline and cause a whole series of physical changes within our bodies, but it can sometimes cause us to do or say things that under ordinary circumstances we might not do.

Perhaps such was the case with Jesus that day when He released His anger with "a scourge of small cords," driving the money changers out of the temple and scattering sheep, oxen, doves, and people in the process. (See John 2:13-17.) The important teaching here, however, is that Jesus got angry and showed it in a demonstration that left no uncertainty in people's minds. This kind of anger is often called "righteous anger."

In this instance, and in other situations where we catch a glimpse of an angry Jesus, we are given an insight into the heart of the Man sent from God. There are those who mistakenly picture Jesus as being "meek and mild." One writer tells of overhearing a woman in a Bible study class say, "I am tired of a little, old, skinny, emaciated Jesus." He was anything but these portrayals.

There are those who struggle with the idea of Jesus being angry. "Isn't this a contradiction of what the Bible says?" they ask. They find it difficult to reconcile one verse in the Bible that tells us not to be angry with other verses that portray an angry God and an angry Jesus.

Each incident in which we see God or Jesus angry must be considered within its context. There is appropriate anger, and there is questionable or inappropriate anger. Malicious, vindictive rage is always inappropriate; we never see God or His Son responding in that way.

A careful study of the various words for "anger" in their original languages sheds light upon this matter. Generally, when the Bible speaks of God's anger, it refers to justified anger and righteous indignation. Many such examples can be found in the Old Testament especially. (See, for instance, Numbers 11:1.) Similar references can be found in the New Testament in such places as Hebrews 3:11, Romans 9:22, and Mark 3:5.

For the Christian who wishes to use anger right, the question uppermost in his thinking must always be: Will this dishonor the Lord and weaken my Christian stance? If so, it would be inappropriate anger. And even if it is right to be angry about something, how I express that anger will largely determine whether I bring dishonor or glory to God.

The Bible gives us guidelines for handling our anger properly. Our feelings and emotions were given to us by the Lord, so in and of themselves they are not sinful. But it is the manner in which they are used that determines the rightness or wrongness of a given emotion.

A good guideline for the Christian to remember is James 1:19: *Let every man be swift to hear, slow to speak, slow to wrath.* (Similar verses can be found in Ecclesiastes

7:9; Proverbs 15:18; Titus 1:7; Psalm 103:8; 145:8; and Nehemiah 9:17.)

When you are tempted to show your anger in an inappropriate way, think of Psalm 37:8: *Cease from anger, and forsake wrath: fret not thyself in any wise to do evil.*

I read recently of a woman who buys chipped china at garage sales for pennies. When her anger and frustration build, she goes into her garage and throws the old cups and plates at the walls. By the time she has vented her anger, she ends up laughing. Doing something physical when we are upset or angry will often clear our bloodstreams of the stimulant the fury produced.

In the case of Jesus showing His anger in the temple, there is general agreement among Bible scholars and others that for Him *not* to have responded to that situation would have been displeasing to the Father. We must recognize that in our own lives, as in Jesus' life, there are times when we may be sinning by *not* getting angry.

Along these lines, Dr. Jack Hayford made this observation:

> To see both sides of Jesus . . . is to see the need for compassion, for care, for concern, for weeping with those that weep, for sympathy, for groaning, for aching deeply because of what you sense transpiring in human lives. And it is to learn the place and time for anger, when we see Satan's wiles successfully destroying; for indignation, when the adversary's program violates territory that is rightfully Christ's; for boldness, when demonic hordes announce their presence; for attack, when the Holy Spirit prompts an advance which faith can make but before which our flesh quails.[1]

---

[1] Dr. Jack Hayford, *Prayer Is Invading the Impossible* (Plainfield, NJ: Logos, 1977), p. 45.

Jesus has appropriately been described as "the Man of Sorrows." Scorned and rejected by His own people, hated and feared by the religious leaders of the day, He was lied about and plotted against. In the end He was betrayed by His own disciple, forsaken by His closest friends, and condemned to death by the very ones He had come to save.

Jesus had a "right" to be hostile. Yet He lived His life without hostility. He taught, *Love your enemies, bless them that curse you, do good to them that hate you, and pray for them which despitefully use you, and persecute you* (Matthew 5:44). On the cross in the midst of the greatest possible physical torment, He prayed, *Father, forgive them; for they know not what they do* (Luke 23:34). Jesus died without hostility.

It is possible that the most personally devastating hurt for Jesus was Peter's denial. The ones who called for His crucifixion didn't know Him. They were motivated out of fear, because He challenged their authority and control over the people. For them, His death was politically expedient rather than a personal matter.

But Peter was a different matter. He had been Jesus' companion, disciple, and friend.

Yet on that blessed morning when the women found the empty tomb, the angel said, *But go your way, tell his disciples **and** Peter that he goeth before you into Galilee: there shall ye see him, as he said unto you* (Mark 16:7).

Jesus knew the emotional anguish Peter was experiencing over what he had done. He could have let him agonize, but instead Jesus singled Peter out in a way that let him know he was forgiven and wanted. "Go tell My disciples and Peter . . . *especially* Peter!"

Jesus returned love for hate, forgiveness for abuse, and life for death. By His Spirit we can and must do the same.

19

Sex and Unprovoked Murder

The human sex drive was divinely given, placed in man and woman by God at the time they were created. It is not dirty and it is not bad. It is good.

Sex is the motivating force and power which guarantees the continuance of the human race. Without it, there would be no human family.

In its divine order, sex is beautiful – a fulfilling experience that can bring great happiness to a man and woman, who have been brought together in the bond of marriage.

Deviate Sex Demands Blood

There is a strong relationship between sex and unprovoked murder, particularly in cases of mass murder.

Almost without exception, people guilty of unprovoked murder are sex misfits. They practice deviate sex and many times are engaged in homosexual activities.

In many of the murder cases set out in chapter 2, the people were involved in deviate sex. This occurs due to the fact that sex in its deviate setting can only be fully consummated with blood.

Deviate sex must have blood. It strives for blood. It cries for blood.

Many times sex maniacs become involved in beatings and other torturous practices. They find sexual gratification by inflicting pain upon other human beings. They hit each other with chains, ropes, and other instruments of torture while engaged in sex – and they call that making

179

love! Pain and torture are a part of their sexual experience. Only the devil could originate such a thing. You can see instantly how abnormal and unnatural this is.

Murder and Sexual Perversion

When a person is yielded to the devil, the ultimate sexual perversion is the taking of blood. The case of John Wayne Gacy in Chicago is a prime example of such perversion.

As we have already discussed in chapter 2, Gacy sexually abused young men and boys, killed them, then buried them under his home. One report stated that he even slept with one of the bodies.

According to Gacy, there were four entities within him. One which he called "Jack" did not like homosexuality. Yet Gacy was driven to commit homosexual acts with his victims before he killed them.

So here is evidence of conflicting demonic personalities: one wanted it, one hated it. But in either situation, the end result was murder. The spirit that demanded sexual perversion also demanded blood.

In many instances men who have committed sex murders cannot give a reason for it. It is a confusing thing to them which shows how the devil has taken over their lives in such a strange way.

Another case that clearly fits this category is the Richard Speck case. (See chapter 2.) The spirit of murder that was in him demanded the blood of innocent women. He forced his way into a nurses' dormitory and killed eight women.

Why?

He had no reason. He didn't know them or anything about them. He says he can't remember all that he did there, but he raped at least one of them. Here again, we see the direct relationship between sex and the destruction of these beautiful young girls.

David Berkowitz, "the Son of Sam," looked for beautiful girls to kill. He said that he liked to work the Queens area of New York City because the girls there were the prettiest. There was a sexual abnormality within him that drove him to take the life of these young girls – girls he had never even seen before. That demonic force within him drove Berkowitz until he had to obey it. He had to destroy lives.

Charles Manson had five women who lived in an almost hypnotic state around him, treating him like a king. They served him in any way he asked. At times, they would be nude as they brought him food and drink, arousing every instinct they could within the man, offering him anything his heart desired.

Sex had a tremendous involvement in the whole Manson situation. The Manson "family" often engaged in a kind of sexual "free for all." They would come together as a group, giving rein to their fleshly desires as they moved from one person to another.

The Preciousness of Sex

What motivates a person to commit sex murders?

I asked the Lord, "Why is it that a man can steal, and people will forgive him; but if he commits adultery, they won't ever forgive him? Why is it that King David committed adultery 3,000 years ago and people still speak against him? If he had stolen a block of gold, nobody would have ever said anything."

The Lord pointed out to me how sex is directly involved in the reproduction of immortal souls. Because of that, God had to place safeguards around it.

Sex is a very precious thing in God's eyes. He created it as an act that is gentle and loving. It is a normal, natural, healthy function of human life. When viewed through God's eyes, it is a holy thing.

That means the devil hates it and will do everything he can to pollute it; to make it dirty, filthy, and unholy; to destroy it. He wants to hurt God in every way possible.

The immoralities of our time are directly related to the satanic influences and powers in our country.

As I often say, there is nothing new about sex. The women in this day do not have one thing that Eve didn't have in the Garden of Eden. To act as if sex today is something new and special is nothing but a fabrication. There is no reality in it whatsoever.

Sex has been with us since the beginning. Multiplied generations of people have been born from it. Why don't we settle down and treat it as it should be treated? If you leave sex as it was created to be, it is divine and beautiful. If you distort it, then it becomes a monstrosity. In our world today, it is a monstrosity.

Jim Jones: A Story of Distorted Sex

The hideous story of Jim Jones and the Peoples Temple tragedy in Guyana, South America, gives clear evidence of how sex can become so distorted.

While in San Francisco, Jones surrounded himself with women. It was reported that he boasted publicly of having had sexual intercourse with all of them; that they begged him for it; and that, at times, he even denied husbands the privilege of touching their own wives.

There is no doubt to me that such behavior only added fuel to the raging fire of filth and degradation within Jim Jones – a "fire" that eventually destroyed 900 lives in one afternoon.

It was reported that Jones was a religious man, but I understand that not one Bible was found in the Jonestown settlement in the Guyana jungle. Jim Jones was not following the Bible. It was not a part of his philosophy.

The Peoples Temple followers were like Marxist revolutionaries. While seeking some sort of socialistic government, they developed only a dictatorship where fear was the ruler. Machine guns were in evidence to keep some of the people from running away.

The Jonestown "massacre" was a very wicked and dreadful thing – and sex was closely related to it all.

Sexual Destruction

Since the sexual desire in humans is so strong, Satan can easily pervert it into a tool of destruction. Because sex is the God-given method of reproduction, Satan wants to use it to destroy. Then he can stand back and laugh at God!

It is the manipulation of the devil that causes human beings to hurt and to destroy one another. Whenever a person permits Satan to dominate his life, it can only lead to destruction.

In the case of the Yorkshire Ripper (see chapter 2), thirteen innocent women were brutally stabbed to death; then their bodies were horribly mutilated. When a person reaches such a place of depravity, only Satan could be responsible. There can be no other reason for such violent and unprovoked destruction of human life.

Consider Ted Bundy

Ted Bundy is a very handsome man, university-trained, intelligent with an I.Q. of over 120, articulate, clean-cut, charming, wholesome in appearance and manner.

But apparently Ted Bundy has a problem. Having been convicted for the murders of three young women in

Florida, he is a top suspect in thirty-six murder cases spanning an area of six states and a period of several years.

The quick verdict in a case such as this would be insanity; but if Bundy is insane, there is very little evidence of it.

His alleged trail through six states left gruesome murder scenes, but very little evidence. It seems that Bundy was always a neat housekeeper, even wiping off fingerprints from some of the apartments and hotel rooms where he stayed.

Ted Bundy has quite a mind, and I find it difficult to consider him "insane" (feebleminded).

Most of the murders to which Bundy is allegedly linked involved sexual assault and abuse. The victims were usually beaten, raped, and strangled. One young girl was sexually assaulted with a bottle. The details are gruesome, but I want you to realize the type of people we are dealing with in these cases.

Can such a person be considered "temporarily insane"?

Is it right for the court to order him to a state mental hospital to live the next years of his life while the real source of the problem goes undiscovered?

The devil is behind the desire within humans to destroy other lives. By becoming the master of a person's life and the energizing force that dominates his being, Satan is able to lead that person to destroy the precious life within other people.

What Can We Do?

It is time that the courts of our land stop and view this situation in the proper light. They have used psychology, psychiatry, and all the methods having to do with human reasoning. Now it is time to consider another course of action.

So you ask, "What can we do?"

The right kind of people can pray for others who are caught in the throes of satanic bondage. They can be set free from that desire for elicit sex and murder.

20

The Fruit of Hostility

Today's hostility, I believe, is a fulfillment of prophecy. Scripture describes the last days preceding Jesus' return as a time of growing hostility, evil, and destruction in the world. We are told that life will be *as the days of Noah* (Matthew 24:37).

Here are some examples of what I believe the Scriptures mean by *as the days of Noah:*

Crime

Crime rates will soar to an uncontrollable high. People will live in fear of their lives, suspiciously guarding themselves not only from strangers but also from neighbors and acquaintances they no longer trust.

Divorce

Divorce statistics will skyrocket, their ever increasing number making a mockery out of the sacred vows meant to last a lifetime. The marriage ceremony will become so meaningless that some people will do away with it altogether, choosing simply to live together.

Sexual Perversion

Sexual perversion will gradually become acceptable under the guise of sexual freedom. Man's thinking will be so tainted and corrupt that he will think it noble to support an individual's right to enter into unnatural relationships. Homosexuality will be widely accepted and even defended as an alternate lifestyle.

Violence

Violence will be a part of everyday life. Wife-beating and child abuse will be epidemic, as will murder, rape, and other forms of destructive behavior.

Practice of the Occult

The practice of the occult, demon worship, and other false religions will become widespread. As they did in the days of Noah, people will turn from God and look to the stars or to their own understanding for the answers to life.

"Wait a minute," you may be saying. "You are not describing some futuristic 'Sodom and Gomorrah' – but my hometown, here and now!"

That's right. The signs are unmistakable. We are living in those last days Jesus spoke about, and the worst times of unleashed hostility are still ahead. That is why it is imperative that we know without a shadow of a doubt how to handle hostility in our lives.

Progress, with all its technological advancements; science, with its theories and formulas; education, with its vast accumulation of knowledge; civilization, with all its sophisticated laws and governing systems – none of these have been able to rid us of the plague of hostility. In fact, in many ways they appear only to have aggravated the problem by giving man a false sense of his own importance. This deceptive feeling of self-sufficiency causes him to rely more and more upon his own abilities and accomplishments and less and less upon God, until the Almighty finally is pushed out of the picture entirely and man becomes his own god.

The Universal Void

This gross impertinence has left man at the mercy of his own weakness and ineptitude and has created an enormous void in his soul. Man was created to have fellowship with God, and without that relationship he is incomplete and constantly searching.

Augustine's well-known statement bears repeating: "Thou madest us for Thyself, and our heart is restless, until it repose in Thee." There is a universal need for God, an incompleteness that only can be met by Him.

People seek to fill this void in all sorts of ways, in order to still the restlessness within their souls.

In many cases, the futility of that search has produced a hostility toward "dead religion," which some men mistakenly equate with a personal relationship with God. In his book, *The Whole Person in a Broken World,* Dr. Paul Tournier writes:

> ... Modern man appears to be disgusted with the religion for which he nevertheless feels a homesickness. He has repressed it, banished it from his life, proclaimed the exclusion of everything beyond the reach of the senses. He has consummated a great rift between the spiritual and the temporal world. And ever since, he has lived in a tragic duality.[1]

This general turn away from organized religion is symbolic of a broader hostility toward all institutions. People who were once regarded with great respect and honor now live in fear of being dragged into court for making mistakes or for not living up to someone else's expectations. Recently a pastor was taken to court by

---

[1]Dr. Paul Tournier, *The Whole Person in a Broken World* (New York: Harper & Row, 1964), n.p.

bereaved parents because his counseling failed to prevent their son from committing suicide. And this is not an isolated case.

Many doctors charge exorbitant fees, not because the cost of medicine is so high but because their insurance rates reflect the number of malpractice suits they may have to defend themselves against. (Of course, where there is legitimate cause, a doctor should be made to pay for his incompetency. But often a lawsuit is merely an expression of rage that a doctor couldn't perform the impossible or be superhuman in his efforts.)

Even teachers are not exempt from this kind of attack from students and irate parents.

Spiritual and Emotional Apathy

The result of all this legal finger-pointing is that people are afraid to get involved. Doctors stand by helplessly and watch an accident victim's life ebb away, knowing that if they try to help and are successful they'll be heroes, but if they fail they'll probably end up in court accused of being little more than murderers.

Some pastors water down their doctrines and rely solely on psychology books when counseling, afraid that declaring the biblical absolutes of right and wrong might offend the current morality.

A friend of mine visited a large, growing church of some renown. He looked with interest at the smiling, well-dressed people hurrying this way and that, while he listened to his host point out the buildings and describe the various programs the church had to offer.

"Well, it all seems to be working," my friend acknowledged. " Everyone certainly seems to have found what they were looking for."

The host replied smugly, "Oh, yes! This isn't like

some other churches I've been to. You can be Buddhist, or
Mormon, or Hindu and feel comfortable here!"

This spiritual and emotional apathy has infected us
all, causing us to draw back at the first sign of trouble or
controversy. We fear the price of involvement will be
more than we want to pay. Even our laws and court systems often seem to penalize the innocent in an attempt to
protect the rights of the guilty. We read in the newspapers
about people sitting by passively listening to pitiful cries
for help just outside their doors. The intensified hostility
of these last days has hardened our hearts and gradually
drained us of compassion for the suffering of others.

Consumer Hostility

Our world lives under the constant harassment of a
contentious spirit that delights in pitting us against one
another. On the whole, society is fearful and untrusting,
constantly expecting the worst instead of the best. We
see this skepticism clearly evidenced by the new "con-
sumerism" that is sweeping the country.

Healthy as it may be in the long run, this consumer
crusade against poor quality and false advertising has
given fresh impetus to a myriad of legal suits in which
manufacturers are threatened with fines or punishments
for the slightest technical infraction, whether it be
because of conflicting government regulations or their
own negligence.

Certainly the consumer has a right to be protected and
a right to the full and prompt redress of his legitimate
grievances. But this right is easily abused and distorted
by turning our courts of law into mere collection agen-
cies. As history has taught us, the only ones to profit from
this proliferation of lawsuits are lawyers.

Another great problem this country faces is the basic

dishonesty our hostility and disrespect for others has created. Insurance companies get cheated out of billions of dollars every year because of fake accidents and false claims. Large companies lose inestimable amounts of money to dishonest employees and executives who think nothing of "padding the expense account a little." Even the most upright citizens find it hard to be totally honest when it comes to filling out their tax forms.

Rebellion Against Authority

All of this is the result of a basic hostility and rebellion against those in authority over us. Since there is no higher authority than God, He has become the object of man's greatest rebellion. There are people who would sue Him if they could!

Not since the days of Noah have men dared to flaunt their hostility and disdain for God so openly. People are no longer brought up to have a healthy respect for God. Where once they questioned quietly in their hearts, they now openly express their contempt and unbelief. The precious name of Jesus is spit out of the mouth of unbelievers in anger more often than it is lovingly spoken by believers in praise and worship.

One of the most common arguments against God today is, "If there is a God, why does He allow all the suffering in the world?" The fact that men blame and curse God instead of looking within themselves and repenting of their evil ways is prophetic. According to the Bible, some people will harden their hearts and refuse to repent right up to the end.

During the time of great Tribulation, the armies of the world will be angry with God.

And the nations were angry, and thy wrath is come,
and the time of the dead, that they should be judged,

and that thou shouldest give reward unto thy servants
the prophets, and to the saints, and them that fear thy
name, small and great; and shouldest destroy them
which destroy the earth.

Revelation 11:18

At one point God will pour out His wrath upon the earth in the form of great plagues and heat.

And men were scorched with great heat, and
blasphemed the name of God, which hath power over
these plagues: and they repented not to give him glory.

Revelation 16:9

People won't think about confessing their sin and getting right with God but will set themselves against Him even more stubbornly and be condemned by their own hostility and unrepentant spirits.

The Disintegration of the Family

When people don't have a healthy relationship with God, their relationships with others soon become perverted. Micah 7:6 predicts what family life will be like just before the Tribulation:

For the son dishonoureth the father, the daughter
riseth up against her mother, the daughter in law against
her mother in law; a man's enemies are the men of his
own house.

How often I hear parents complain of this very thing. "My children have no respect for what I am and what I stand for. They want to do things their way. They don't listen anymore!"

The disintegration of the family is already of great concern to those who understand its dire implications. We live in a world where maternal and paternal instinct are more matters of choice than natural responses. A new life is assigned little or no value; if it is inconvenient it is readily aborted or disowned at birth. It has even been proposed by certain humanists that parents should be given three days after the birth of a baby to decide whether or not they want to keep it. If not, it would be "humanely" disposed of.

Many children grow up feeling like interruptions in their parents' lives, while parents struggle pathetically to gain their children's love and respect without investing the necessary time and discipline. The trend of role reversal between mothers and fathers, the strong effort of some to erase sexual definitions, the increase in divorce, and the introduction of the homosexual "family unit" have steadily eaten away at the foundations of traditional family life.

This erosion of family relationships is resulting in more and more incidents like the one reported on recent newscasts about a twelve-year-old girl who set her parents' bed on fire in the middle of the night. Another young man kept his elderly mother virtually prisoner in her own home, physically and verbally abusing her until neighbors finally reported their suspicions to the police and the young man was arrested.

Hostility within the family unit will grow in intensity until Jesus returns; only those relationships based on the principles of God's Word will be capable of natural expressions of love, respect, and loyalty.

Hostility Between Management and Labor

In the last days management and labor are going to be in deadly contest. We see the first stirrings of this conflict in the massive move toward socialism throughout the world. Even here in the United States, which was founded upon the concepts of free enterprise and democracy, we find a growing socialist tendency influencing our thinking and even creeping into our politics.

But neither socialism nor any other form of government can solve the world's problems, because it is impossible to abolish hatred, greed, and hostility from men's hearts through legislation. When men refuse to acknowledge their sin, they look elsewhere for a logical scapegoat.

The Antichrist

Deceptions will increase as the world prepares for the appearance of the Antichrist. Daniel 8:23-25 describes Daniel's vision of the end times:

And in the latter time of their kingdom, when the transgressors are come to the full, a king of fierce countenance, and understanding dark sentences, shall stand up.

Verse 23

This verse refers to the Antichrist. He will be a man who has an answer for everything.

And his power shall be mighty, but not by his own power: and he shall destroy wonderfully, and shall prosper, and practice, and shall destroy the mighty and the holy people.

Verse 24

The Antichrist will have demonic power to support him, and he will desire to destroy the Jewish people.

And through his policy also he shall cause craft to prosper in his hand; and he shall magnify himself in his heart, and by peace shall destroy many: he shall also stand up against the Prince of princes; but he shall be broken without hand.

Verse 25

The Antichrist will bring prosperity to the whole world for a time, and men will say, "Who is like this one? Let us serve him!" (See Revelation 13:4.) He will control the United Nations, and he will destroy the entire world. At the appointed time, when wickedness is at its peak, a man will come whose fierceness will be felt by all the inhabitants of the earth.

In the last days the devil will actually walk the earth, with great wrath.

Therefore rejoice, ye heavens, and ye that dwell in them. Woe to the inhabiters of the earth and of the sea! for the devil is come down unto you, having great wrath, because he knoweth that he hath but a short time.

Revelation 12:12

At this time hostility will be at its peak. People will be the victims not only of their own hostility but also of Satan's anger. The resultant upheaval will be so great that Matthew 24:22 says, *Except those days should be shortened, there should no flesh be saved: but for the elect's sake those days shall be shortened.*

Just at the point when hostility is about to destroy mankind completely, Jesus will return.

And I saw heaven opened, and behold a white horse; and he that sat upon him was called Faithful and True, and in righteousness he doth judge and make war . . .

And he was clothed with a vesture dipped in blood: and his name is called The Word of God . . .

And he hath on his vesture and on his thigh a name written, KING OF KINGS, AND LORD OF LORDS.

Revelation 19:11,13,16

Only Christ, the King of kings, will destroy hostility and its direct cause – Satan.

In speaking of the last days, Jesus said:

Now learn a parable of the fig tree; when his branch is yet tender, and putteth forth leaves, ye know that summer is nigh:

So likewise ye, when ye shall see all these things, know that it is near, even at the doors.

Matthew 24:32,33

Let us open our eyes and our minds to recognize just where we are in the course of history. The Bible says that in the last days there will be a great falling away. But it also says that God will pour out His Spirit upon all flesh. Our heart attitudes will decide whether we will be susceptible to deception or available to that outpouring of the Holy Spirit.

21
Prophecy and Unprovoked Murder

Prophecy has to do with the fulfillment of history. When it is spoken beforehand that a certain event will come to pass, and that event does come to pass, prophecy is fulfilled.

When I was a boy, it was said that crime would cease when everybody was educated. They said that since crime had to do with ignorance and with poverty, once the people had a good education and were making money, there would be no more reason for crime.

Even preachers were saying this. They thought that when ignorance and poverty were taken care of, society would be well on its way to utopia. But suddenly they realized that conditions were becoming worse than ever.

You could probably start a university within the walls of our federal prisons in America, because of the number of college professors and qualified teachers found there. Though a man is tremendously accelerated in mental knowledge, he is not always made better morally.

The First Murder

After Adam and Eve had openly rebelled against God and were driven from the Garden of Eden, the first great sin recorded was the sin of fratricide – the act of a brother killing a brother. Cain murdered Abel.

The disagreement which created the atmosphere for this first murder was not regarding food, or real estate, or precious jewels, or personal honor and prestige. It had to do with religion, a subject that has caused enormous controversy and strife among men ever since.

Both brothers wanted to be accepted by God, but only one gained that acceptance. Each brother brought his sacrifice before the Lord, but only one was found acceptable in God's eyes. When Abel's sacrifice was received by God, Cain became angry, so he rose up and slew his brother.

Abel did not provoke Cain to commit murder. He was simply worshiping God, but his brother could not accept that. When anger and jealousy rose up within Cain, Satan took advantage of it and led Cain to commit an act of murder.

God, responding to this emotional and satanic deed committed by Cain, said to him, *The voice of thy brother's blood crieth unto me from the ground* (Genesis 4:10).

Blood has a language.

God could hear Abel's blood crying out to be avenged. He had to do something about it, so He placed a curse upon Cain.

Murder Prophesied

This first case of unprovoked murder should be noted very carefully in man's destiny. Murder has been in the world ever since.

The Bible reveals many terrible incidents of one human being maliciously taking the life of another.

According to biblical prophecy, in the last days, preceding the Great Tribulation and at the time of the rapture of the saints, murder will be at a greater degree of prevalence than it has ever been in the history of the world.

We have now reached those final days of God's

Dispensation of Grace. Before we enter into the Great Tribulation period, there will be an acceleration of murder.

Perhaps we should view the increase of murder as a prophetic sign that Jesus is coming soon.

Perhaps it should stir our hearts to get right with God, to seek the Lord while He may be found and call upon Him while He is near. (Isaiah 55:6.)

James, the brother of our Lord Jesus Christ, wrote a message to the Church in the New Testament. He speaks of the Last Days in chapter 5. In verse 6 he cites one of the conditions that would be present at that time: *Ye have condemned and killed the just; and he doth not resist you.*

We are seeing this very thing in the world today. Just in the atheistic countries throughout the world where Communism reigns, many innocent and godly people have been condemned and killed. The lives of men, women, and children have been mercilessly destroyed because of the way they chose to think and live.

A spirit of murder is upon the face of this earth. People are killed without having offered resistance.

For the people responsible for these millions of lives that have been lost, God has a day of reckoning.

These are the last days. We are living in a moment of prophecy. There will be gross multiplication of people who will lose their lives through murder. Totally without cause, people will be killing other people.

In verse 8 of James, chapter 5, God says to His people who love Him: *Be ye also patient; stablish your hearts: for the coming of the Lord draweth nigh.*

In the midst of the sin and slaughter, God admonishes us to be patient and look for the coming of the Lord.

The Horsemen in Revelation

The Revelation of St. John, the last book of the Bible,

prophesies of more slaughter than the world has ever known. It will be a frightening situation.

Chapter 6 tells of things that will surely come to pass. It describes the problems coming to the earth as resembling horsemen.

The first horseman (v. 2) is riding a white horse and represents world leadership without war. The second horseman (v. 4) is sitting upon a red horse, which speaks of war.

In both cases the rider is the same person – the Antichrist – only he has changed his stance. First, he was a man of peace, then he became a man of war. This verse says he will "take peace from the earth" and people will kill one another. This will be the beginning of the greatest carnage mankind has ever known.

There will not be a lessening of murder, only an increase.

I urge you to read the entire chapter; then read chapters 8 and 9 to see what will be taking place just after the Church is raptured, after the good people have gone to heaven.

The fourth horseman (v. 8) is riding a pale horse. The white horse was the horse of peace. The red horse was the horse of war. The pale horse is the horse of death.

This fourth horseman, riding a pale horse, will go out to kill one-fourth of the earth's population with the sword. This will be a result, not of war, but of anger and hatred within the people.

The spirit of murder will be so prevalent within people that one-fourth of the world's population will be destroyed. If there are four billion people living today, that means there would be one billion human beings killed! This is really beyond human comprehension – a slaughter the world has never known.

The War of Wars

Chapter 9 tells how the Antichrist, empowered by the devil, will gather together an army of fighting men. Verse 16 says, *And the number of the army of the horsemen were two hundred thousand thousand.*

The war that comes at that time will cause the destruction of one-third of all men.

Verse 18 says they will be destroyed by the fire, the smoke, and the brimstone: The fire comes from heaven; the smoke comes up from the earth; the brimstone comes out of hell. At the junction of these three, one-third of all mankind shall die.

The world has not known war and death as it will be known at that time.

Prophecy Fulfilled

Verse 20 says, *And the rest of the men which were not killed by these plagues yet repented not of the works of their hands. . . .* These people will see all the devastation, but still will not repent of their works.

The first of these "works" is: *. . . that they should not worship devils.* This prophecy reveals how people, more and more, are going to worship devils. They will become involved in spiritism and occultism. They will delve into the Oriental philosophies. All of this, involving demon worship, will continue to be accepted.

Verse 20 says they will worship devils and have idols of gold, silver, brass, stone, and wood.

Verse 21 says, *Neither repented they of their murders.*

We are seeing this scripture fulfilled today in such horrible cases of mass murder. Most of these men are not sorry for what they did.

When asked, "Are you sorry?" they answer without emotion, "No. I did what I had to do."

The devil told them to do it, so they did it.

Neither repented they of their murders, nor their sorceries [spiritism and occultism], *nor of their fornication* [sexual immoralities] *nor of their thefts* (v. 21). Some people today will kill just to steal fifty cents!

The sins that are prevalent today are the sins of the Great Tribulation period that is coming upon this world. I am very plainly revealing to you a picture of the world – as it is today, and as it will be.

Mankind is headed into the Great Tribulation. But we don't have to go. Nobody has to go. We can look up, call on God through Jesus Christ, and be saved from the things that will be coming to pass. That is the reason The Revelation was written: so we can read it and be saved from the things coming upon the earth.

The Bible gives a clear description of how things will be at some time in the future. Revelation 22:14,15 says:

Blessed are they that do his commandments, that they may have right to the tree of life, and may enter in through the gates into the city.

For without are dogs, and sorcerers, and whore-mongers, and murderers, and idolaters, and whosoever loveth and maketh a lie.

All these people – sorcerers, whoremongers, murderers, idolators, who love and make a lie – will never get inside the gates of heaven. They will be forbidden entry into heaven forever.

The Lord Jesus said in John 16:2, *Whosoever killeth you will think that he doeth God service.* The time will come when people will kill good people and think they have done God a service and have done the will of God. They will say, "I did it for God's sake. I did it to show how good I was."

In the times in which we live today, there are many

far-fetched religious ideas in circulation. I urge you to give heed to what the Bible says for the Bible is the truth of God.

God's Word says in James 4:2, *Ye lust, and have not: ye kill, and desire to have, and cannot obtain.* There is no one who kills for satisfaction and gets it. A person may kill, thinking, *I'm going to have fulfillment. This will give me what I need.* But that is impossible.

Killing has never brought fulfillment and satisfaction. Fulfillment comes from loving God, from serving God, and living before Him.

Only love – nothing else – can bring fulfillment to our lives.

People who kill are seeking to have peace within themselves, to find fulfillment, but God's Word tells us that a murderer will never have fulfillment.

A Spirit of Murder

I heard this testimony of an ex-Chief of Police:

"There was a time when I could sit down and eat a meal with a man sitting across the table from me. I could get angry at that man, take out my gun, shoot him dead, lay the gun on the table, finish eating my food, get up, go home, undress, go to bed, and sleep well. I had a spirit of murder in me; but when Jesus came into my heart, He took that spirit of murder from me."

There is a spirit of murder operating in the lives of multiplied thousands of people today. Some have actually committed murder; many others have wanted to kill, but didn't. Perhaps they were afraid. Maybe they didn't have the opportunity. In either case, the desire was already in their hearts.

I cannot tell you, prophetically speaking, that the

world is going to get better. I cannot tell you that you are going to be safer than you were before. I can only say what God's prophetic Word says and warn you about that which is to come.

Prophetically, we are living very close to the Second Coming of the Lord Jesus Christ. Unprovoked murder will become more prevalent in the world. Without rhyme or reason, people will continue to destroy the lives of innocent men, women, and children.

If there was ever a time when men need to seek God, that time is today.

If there was ever a time when human beings need to know the peace of God in their hearts, it is today.

About the Author
Dr. Lester Sumrall

The voice of Dr. Lester Sumrall remains prominent in the Christian world today. More than 65 years of ministry in over 100 nations made Dr. Sumrall a respected source of wisdom and understanding. He was an author, teacher, missionary, evangelist, and the pastor and founder of Christian Center Cathedral of Praise in South Bend, Indiana. In 1957, he founded LeSEA, a multi-faceted global outreach.

Today LeSEA's outreaches include television, satellite, FM and shortwave radio, and **LeSEA Global Feed The Hungry**. Throughout his lifetime, Dr. Sumrall worked tirelessly to fulfill the Great Commission by carrying the gospel to the ends of the earth.

About LeSEA Global Feed The Hungry

LeSEA Global Feed The Hungry was created in 1987 to feed the hungry around the world and provide emergency relief to those in need as a result of famine, drought, flood, war or other disasters. Our mission is simple . . . to show God's compassion to people in need, to bless "forgotten" members within the body of Christ, to strengthen the church and evangelize the lost. We are a pastor to pastor, church to church program by which supplies are given to leaders within the church or church community who in turn give to those experiencing need.

Why is LeSEA Global Feed The Hungry so dedicated to the poor and hurting? One reason is because there is great need in our world. It is estimated that one billion people (most of whom are children) live in hunger. However, the primary motive for our dedication is obedience to the Word of God. Those who have this world's goods are instructed to bless those who have not (1 Timothy 6:17-19).

"It wasn't by accident that I was awakened at midnight in Jerusalem in 1987. God wanted to speak to me. He let me know that Christians who had no food were praying, 'give us this day or daily bread.' Our efforts are simply to put bread in their mouths."

Lester Sumrall

LeSEA World Harvest Prayerline

Realizing people's need for direction and encouragement could happen at any time of the day or night, LeSEA established "Prayerline." Dedicated, trained volunteers man the phones 24-hours a day, and are ready to pray and encourage people during their time of need. LeSEA's Prayerline can be reached at (219) 291-1010. or via the Internet at www.worldharvest.com.

Other Books by Dr. Lester Sumrall

101 QUESTIONS & ANSWERS ON DEMON POWERS
60 THINGS GOD SAID ABOUT SEX
ADVENTURING WITH CHRIST
ANGELS TO HELP YOU
BE BOLD AND WALK TALL
BITTEN BY DEVILS
COURAGE TO CONQUER
DARK HOLE OF WORLD HUNGER
DEMONS, THE ANSWER BOOK
EXORCISM
GIFTS & MINISTRIES OF THE HOLY SPIRIT
HOW TO KNOW THE WILL OF GOD
LIFE STORY OF LESTER SUMRALL
MAKING OF A CHAMPION
MILITANT CHURCH
MY THREE SONS
NAMES OF GOD
OVERCOMING COMPULSIVE DESIRES
PAUL, MAN OF THE MILLENNIUM
PIONEERS OF FAITH
PROMISES OF GOD
REALITY OF ANGELS
RUN WITH VISION
SPIRIT, SOUL AND BODY
SUPERNATURAL PRINCIPALITIES & POWERS
UNPROVOKED MURDER
VICTORY & DOMINION OVER FEAR
YOU CAN DESTROY THE GATES OF HELL

For more information or for a catalog write:
Sumrall Publishing • P.O. Box 12 • South Bend, IN 46624